# START WITH YOUR GIFT

# START WITH YOUR GIFT

## UNDERSTAND AND MONETIZE IT WHILE SERVING OTHERS

FRED OPIE

Published by Opie Press
Natick, MA 01760
www.FredOpie.com

First published 2017

Manufactured in the United States

ISBN 978-0-9991893-0-6

Library of Congress Control Number: 2017910657

This publication is designed to provide essential and researched information with regard to the subject discussed. It is published with the understanding that the publisher is not engaged in rendering financial, accounting, or other professional advice. If financial advice or other expert assistance is required, professional services are advised.

Cover Design: DesignStudio

Interior Design: Tracy Quinn McLennan and Allan Ytac

# CONTENTS

# INTRODUCTION

Young athletes often look at college and professional players as talented people who have depended on God-given gifts to excel in their sport. Over the course of my playing, coaching, and teaching experience, I have observed that this is a big and bold myth! Talent on the field and in life excels in the first quarter and may endure until the second quarter. But it gives out in the second half, and the athletes with talent *and discipline* thrive, particularly in the second half of competition and life.

*That's me on the right giving teammate, Dan Pratt, a high five after scoring a goal in the 1985 NCAA Division 1 National Championship against Johns Hopkins. Hopkins went on to defeat us for the second time in a row in the finals. I would trade that goal for a national championship any day!*

I have seen too many talented athletes who never acquired the ingredients for success (integrity, effort, and care) and, consequently, lose out on so many great opportunities. I'm a former Syracuse University (SU) and US National Team athlete. Every time I see a college team competing on television, I think about the fact that, more than likely, I'm not seeing their best competing on the team's roster. Their best players may not even be watching from the sideline. Some of the best players in terms of talent lacked the emotional maturity and discipline to get their act together and give their best effort to make it onto the field or court. The athletes who get playing time are those who have learned how to make good choices, work hard, and care about others.

As a high school senior applying to colleges, I received one rejection letter after another, and, consequently, I became depressed. I felt like a failure. Great athletes also experience a similar depression when their playing careers come to a slow or sudden end. For the first time in decades, they have had to think about life after sports—something that great athletes often resist contemplating. When you're good, you feel invincible until you experience a career-ending injury or the powers that be decide you're overpaid or underperforming and release you.

I had to learn some hard lessons such as starting out with understanding who God created me to be and what gifts he put on the inside of me. It took a long time for me to come to that understanding, but this book, if you read it carefully, can keep you from being a wandering generality and/or great athlete focused on obtaining superficial goals such as wins, championships, and individual honors such as All-American status and inductions to Halls of Fame. If you have the genetics, work ethic, and the opportunity to play on a great team you will more than likely achieve the accolades just mentioned. However, it is not going to fill the hole in your soul that comes from the pursuit of personal gain and the myth of more—more wins, more accolades, more money, more degrees and titles, and more pleasure.

I hit my stride in life later than you should have to after I made the choice to focus on growing and maturing on a daily basis and understanding the importance of diligence, which I define as a consistent movement toward excellence. Now let me be clear: I am focused on obtaining excellence in each and everything I do in life with the understanding that I'm a human being with all kinds of frailties and imperfections. But I'm going to grow more and enjoy more as a person aiming for excellence than the person that aims for nothing or little that is excellent. If you aim for nothing you will hit it every time!

This book is my attempt to get the younger version of me to stop acting like normal people who are spending too much time and money on sports. In this book, I unpack my thoughts and decisions over five decades as a person who has been embedded in youth, high school, and college education and athletics. As journalists have been embedding themselves in military units in Iraq and Afghanistan, I similarly have done the same in athletics and education. We need to stop the madness and focus on first things first. That is what gift God placed in you to be of service to others and to make an income. It is the best place and space to develop your gift. I am convinced that that is the most appropriate recipe for living and giving and having a great and impacting life in the process.

I talk openly about my faith in this book because it's a central part of who I am and my journey, and it may or may not be the same with you. You don't have to be a person of faith to benefit from reading the book. In fact, I invite you to skip the sections of the book in which I share my faith as well as scriptures relevant to a point if that works for you. I don't want to force you to believe what I believe or how I believe. The best way I can explain it is you can't get into water without getting wet and I can't explain what I've learned that has led me to write this book without occasionally sharing about my faith. What I've written is a recipe book for making well-adjusted people who, I would argue, are somewhat of an endangered species. Maybe you do, but I don't know many well-adjusted people who are excelling on and off the field and don't need to abuse drugs and/or alcohol to cope with the challenges of life that come to us all. This is a recipe book for finding a vocation that feels like a vacation and one for great athletes long after their playing days are over. If you are a great athlete, enjoy the season of competition that you're in and then prepare for an even more enjoyable life thereafter. Getting released and/or fired can be a great opportunity to enter a career doing the kind of work you have been gifted to do. This is a story of how I developed this recipe first in my own life. As you will read, just like any good baker, I made lots of bad batches of cookies before I perfected the recipe. If you had success, you need to reflect and document what you did so that you can repeat the outcome as well as improve on it.

There are several themes that you'll see throughout this book. First, it's a look at the journey to developing the recipe I am sharing in this book. I invite you into the multiple locker rooms of my life, sharing some of my biggest mistakes and worst decisions so that you don't have to make them in your own life. Second, you'll get my halftime speeches so you can get your life on track to achieve what you want on and off the field or court. Third, you'll read about my car, which serves as a metaphor for my working career.

My journey can best be described as periods in which I needed an engine overhaul, regular maintenance, roadside assistance, and realignments.

I share tips in which I sincerely hope you'll take out your pen and make notes on the page and in the margins to get the most out of what I'm sharing. I'm going to recommend books for you to read that I have gleaned from in preparing this book. Go to your local library or purchase them.

What I have written here is designed to be a recipe book to make over your life and get you to the place where you know what your gifts are, you've surrounded yourself with great mentors, you're plugged into the right type of training for using your gifts, you work the plan (including getting a great internship), and you're on the road in the vehicles/jobs that get you to the place you want to be five to ten years from now.

Once you get to the point where the recipe is producing great results in your life, I want you to live and give back like nobody else. I want you to make an impact on the world around you by paying back everything you've learned from taking a deep dive into this book and using the ingredients in the recipe. I worked the recipe and the recipe has worked for me, so it can work for you if you put it to work and trust the process. Eighty percent of the reason why successful people get ahead is the effort and focus they have in their life. The other 20 percent comes from the gifts and abilities that God gives to each of us. So, what am I saying? Focus on the 80 percent you can control and stop making excuses for failures that you're wallowing in now.

I have been on teams with losing seasons and on teams with winning seasons. Winning is a whole lot better! One of my favorite scriptures is Hosea 4:6, which tells me what you don't know can destroy you. Knowing how to do better is part of the process of winning in life: It's closely associated with choosing to learn valuable insights and apply them to one's life. But the opposite is also true. Think about it. What you don't know can destroy you, cause you to lose, and it keep you from ever getting ahead in life! That says to me that you want to put a premium on obtaining knowledge and wisdom.

What's the difference between knowledge and wisdom? Knowledge is information, and wisdom is the ability to apply it in every decision you make in life. *Life is full of decisions that can cause you to get ahead or cause you to fall behind.* A definition of wisdom that I heard Senior Pastor Tim Keller of Redeemer Presbyterian Church in New York City share in a series of sermons he did on the book of Proverbs that I like is, *Wisdom is knowing how things really work and are and what to do because of those insights.*

What you're about to read will only give you the ability to make over being ignorant, which, in my book, means being unaware. You need to move beyond knowing the right thing to do and make a conscious decision to *do* the right thing. The rejection of knowledge is a sad thing. As Maya Angelou once said, "When you know better, you can do better."

Another one of my favorite scriptures is Romans 10:17, which tells me that *faith*—the unlimited, inexhaustible power of God—comes from hearing the word of God and hearing it over and over and over again—I can change myself for the better. I can transform my stinking thinking so that I have a renewed ability to make wise choices (see Romans 12:1-2). If I can change how I think for the better, that truly is a miracle! I can change how I view problems and situations that I don't like and focus on what I can impact instead of having a pity party about the impact of others on me. I learned that with God all things are possible, including changing the recipe I have been using to make short- and long-term decisions in my life about my career (see Matthew 19:26).

I'm an auditory learner, so I took Romans 10:17 to heart and committed to hearing the word of God day and night to build the kind of faith necessary to change my thinking and, as a result, the outcomes in my life. I'm not asking you to do the same unless you want the results you will read about in this book. The minute I hit the ground in the morning, I plug my headset into my smartphone, turn the Bible app on, and start listening to and hearing the word of God. Why? Because I believe the nugget of truth, "garbage in, garbage out" and, conversely, *"wisdom in, wisdom out."*

I learned long ago that the Bible calls the word of God the wisdom of God. Think about that. By listening to the word of God first thing in the morning, I'm filling myself with the wisdom of the God of the universe! That's an awesome thought to me. What is the first thing you listen to when you get up? What do you fill yourself up with right *before* you go to bed? Is it uplifting or is it depressing; is it inspiring or is it discouraging? We are, in many regards, the totality of what we hear and choose to believe.

We've all had the experience of driving past a recently killed skunk. Skunks have a protective strategy—a gland that allows them to spray a terribly pungent and awful odor that repels their adversaries. When a car runs over the skunk and ruptures that gland, even if you don't drive directly over the skunk your car becomes doused with that odor, and it stinks to high heaven! Similarly, when you allow yourself to be around negative content, particularly first thing in the morning and before going to bed, your thoughts become stinking thinking. And we act based on what we think, both positively and negatively.

This recipe book is for those who want to join a special forces unit in life—a civilian version of the Army Rangers or the Navy SEALs. We need some folks committed to making a positive impact on the world around us, particularly in the world of sports. The image we are getting today of athletes is nuts, and the examples they're setting are contributing to the problems around us, because people follow athletes, whether we like it or not.

Follow the recipe in this cookbook if you're interested in producing better results in your life and making a difference. If not, leave this book on the shelf and give somebody else the opportunity to read it.

As you will see, I love sayings, quotes, and mantras, so here's a question to live by: *Do you want to be comfortable or do you want to be committed?*

Fred Opie
Natick, Massachusetts
2017

# CHAPTER 1

# Recognizing Your Gift

You may have low self-esteem from the failure you have experienced to this point in your life, but I'm here to tell you that God doesn't make mistakes, and he has given you—yes, you!—a very special gift that makes you unique and distinctive. A gift that gives you the ability to stand out, to be outstanding. But the problem is that many of us have been wallowing around in life with that sad sack over our heads, feeling sorry for ourselves because we think we don't have a gift. You do have a gift. The fact that you haven't recognized it yet, exercised it, and developed it doesn't mean that you don't have one. I repeat: You have a gift from God that we need! Ephesians 4:8, 1 Timothy 4:14, and 2 Timothy 1:6 clearly show that God has given you a gift; however, it is up to you to activate that gift and not neglect it. We'll talk more about how to activate and develop it later in the book.

It's been my observation that athletes tend to focus on their athletic gifts and overlook nonathletic gifts. It's like the folks I see in some weight rooms who have great upper bodies but continue to focus on their upper-body muscles and neglect their lower-body muscles. Here's my theory on why athletes don't develop their nonathletic gifts: it's because, as humans, we have a need for praise. We naturally go in the direction where we receive it the most. Often, fathers are guilty for allowing this to happen in their children, particularly their male children. As Joe Ehrmann discusses in his book, *InSideOut Coaching*, men have been socialized to associate masculinity with three things—athletic ability, sexually exploiting women, and wealth. As Joe puts it, older men, particularly professional athletes, influence us to focus on achieving on the ball field, in the bedroom, and the billfold (a wallet full with money).[1] We focus on athletic performance to the neglect of other areas of our lives. It's unfortunate but true. If you don't think so, go to a middle school athletic event and then go to a middle school theater event, spelling bee, or other nonathletic event. You will see dozens of fathers attending the athletic event and predominately women at the nonathletic events. This is true of dads living in the same house with their children and dads living outside the home of their children.

Dr. Kevin Leman's book *Planet Middle School* describes a time in our life in which so many changes are happening, in addition to going through puberty.[2] I attended Pierre Van Cortlandt Middle School in my hometown of Croton-on-Hudson, New York, about thirty-five miles north of New York City. Middle school was tough for me. An experience that remains etched in my mind is Spanish class. I give the teacher the benefit of the doubt that he did not mean to shame me in front of my peers, time after time asking me questions that, in my view, confirmed just how little Spanish I knew, but that's what it felt like. He would ask me a question in Spanish that I did not understand and that made me feel like fleeing. As soon as I could, I dropped the class, immaturely avoiding another challenge. What's funny is that to earn a PhD in history I had to learn Spanish! I learned to love it and later became proficient.

School officials in my school district and my parents did what they thought right to help me as a child with attention deficit disorder (ADD). I received a diagnosis around 1973. At the same time, I lacked the maturity to work hard and seek help with my schoolwork, choosing instead to take the road of least resistance. As author Simon Sinek puts it, I didn't have a *why* to give me the power of purpose to plow through the difficult moments that come while completing homework assignments and exams.[3] Meanwhile, I had a love of sports that allowed me to push through and read, for example, all the content the Croton Free Library had about hockey. As I have gotten older, I've realized that one of my gifts is the ability to do research.

In middle school I started watching ice hockey during the height of Hall of Famer Bobby Orr's career with the Boston Bruins.[4] Watching him sparked my short-lived hockey career, which started in a house league hosted at the now-defunct Westchester Skating Rink in Hawthorne, New York. I played hockey from the sixth grade until my senior year in high school. Some of you are questioning, you grew up playing hockey? A black kid growing up playing hockey sounds just as crazy as southerner Dave

Ramsey who also grew up playing hockey in Tennessee and both are true. The frequent 6:00 a.m. ice times that required me to get up on my own at 5:00 a.m., wake my parents up, and get my gear on and into the car instilled a self-discipline that continues to benefit me today. In addition, the eye, hand, talk, and stick skills I acquired playing hockey, I would argue, made me a better lacrosse player, particularly with ground balls. By the way, lacrosse is Canada's national sport—not hockey. The games complement each other. I still skate today but no longer play lacrosse.[5]

Thanks to hockey I developed excellent research and study skills! And here's the point: love for something gives us the ability to push through difficulties. As early as you can identify the things that are legal and moral that you love, learn more about them. Ultimately, my love for sports gave me the ability to work hard in college, which allowed me to remain eligible to play the game I loved. Later, after about age twenty-five, my frontal cortex became fully functional, and I had the ability to understand the importance of education. Before then, I could not have cared less for school except for the fact that it was necessary to be eligible to play lacrosse.

It's been my observation that we, as young adults, in most instances, don't lack the ability to do well in school. *Many of us lack an understanding of why we should take school seriously and give our best effort,* and we don't have the love of learning necessary to make it through the highs and lows that happen in the process of learning. Secondly, in this quick-fix culture we live in, *most of us need training to develop great work habits.* We need to understand that *constructive criticism is part of the formula of succeeding in life.* I've seen this during my twenty-plus years of teaching and coaching. In armed combat in Afghanistan or Iraq as a member of the US Armed Forces, getting shot is one of the reasons you later get medals, but we live in a world in which people want medals but don't want to get shot.

## Recognizing Your Gift

What do you do that's off the hook and you barely break a sweat in the process? A gift is not limited to sports and entertainment. There are many other options. Can you make a meal out of virtually nothing in the refrigerator? Are you able to walk into a situation that others see as hopeless and see great opportunities? Do you have the ability to give advice to friends who are confused about what to do next in life and clearly point out the helpful path ahead? Are you a great listener? Can you organize a room in

9

disarray? Do you love animals? Can you build websites? Are you great at building things with your hands or inventing things? Do you love working out and showing others how to get in shape? Do you love negotiating and/or settling disputes? Do you love giving manicures and pedicures? Can you easily take electronic gadgets apart and put them back together? Do you love designing logos? Do love travel? Do you enjoy camping and roughing it? What is it that God has gifted you to do and enjoy? When we use our gift to serve others we feel satisfaction while receiving compensation in the process.[6]

Here's what I've learned over the years: my job is not my gift. It is a place where I use my gift. Second, I use my gift in many aspects of my life, including in my relationships with other people. My gift has always been with me but I have not always been aware of it. It was there on my first day of school many years ago and when we moved from one community to another. It was there when I graduated from high school but I still had no clue what it was and how to monetize it. And even when I didn't understand it my gift existed because I did. My gift and your gift is bigger than a single job. My unique gift has and your gift will make room for you in numerous spaces and places.[7] For example, after I came to the knowledge of my gift of teaching and coaching, it started making room for me in and all kinds of situation circumstances. It gave me invitations to use it in schools; at banquets and conferences; in articles, books, newspapers, and magazines; on podcast, radio, and television. When I'm on TV, I'm teaching people. When I'm coaching, I'm teaching people. When I'm in a documentary film, I'm teaching people. When I'm on a podcast, I'm teaching people. When I'm on YouTube, I'm teaching people. When I'm on the History Channel, I'm teaching people. I take my gift with me wherever I go and I use it to open doors to opportunities to serve others and earn an income. Often, I use my gift for free to serve others and have an impact on the world around me.

Ken Coleman, author of *One Question: Life-Changing Answers from Today's Leading Voices,* and Christie Wright, the author of *Business Boutique: A Woman's Guide for Making Money Doing What She Loves,* provide excellent suggestions on how to learn what your gift is. Coleman suggests that we make the following list:

1. The top three things you do best
2. Get feedback from your first list from three people who know you best
3. List what you value, talk about, and do the most
4. List three ways you can act on what you learn from your list

10

Christie Wright uses five questions to help people understand their gift:

1. What do you enjoy?
2. What is effortless for you?
3. Where do you excel in relationship to other people?
4. What gives you energy?
5. What do others encourage in you?

The ability to do research easily and enjoy the process is one of my gifts. Most of us have one or two primary gifts and talents and one or two secondary gifts and talents. My second primary gift is teaching and coaching. Throughout my youth sports experience and as a high school athlete, I was never selected as a team captain. However, by my senior year in high school, my gift as a teacher began pouring out of my mouth. My high school lacrosse teammate, Ed Podhast, sarcastically gave me the nickname coach because I spent so much time during practice and games trying to instruct teammates on how to play.

Years later a roommate came home late one evening. My door was closed and the light was on in my room. From my room, he heard what sounded like I was teaching a class. When I opened the door and came out, he peeked into my room to see who was there; to his surprise, it was empty. I had created a teaching outline and had been recording content. I was putting my teaching gift in motion and visualizing that I was standing before a packed auditorium teaching people. I did that several times and still have the recordings that I listen to from time to time. Just yesterday morning, I gave such a talk in a college auditorium to a group of student athletes.

In terms of sports, early in my life I learned that I had an above-average sports aptitude that included a competitive nature, drive, eye-hand coordination, and a love of competition that made practicing against better opponents a pleasure instead of a pain. *A commitment to getting better and the drive to do so is a hallmark of gifted athletes who experience achievement beyond sandlot ball and recreation leagues.* Throughout my life, I've struggled with being too competitive when playing games and turning off my teacher speak when I'm not called on to teach. What I'm saying is that every gift and talent pushed to its extreme irritates those around us, particularly our family, friends, and teammates.

As I mentioned, I grew up in a village called Croton-on-Hudson, a beautiful suburb of New York City on the Hudson River. There were acres of woods around my house and I explored as much of them as I could before the land became overdeveloped with houses. These enjoyable experiences in the woods led me to think about becoming a forest ranger. As I had been in the habit of doing from a very young age, I went to our local public library and started doing research on that career. Keep in mind that I was doing this as an elementary school child. In eighth or ninth grade, I had the opportunity to work as a member of a youth conservation corps, a government program that put youth to work maintaining state parks throughout Westchester County, where I lived. The experience of working in the heat and in close proximity to hungry mosquitoes changed my mind about becoming a ranger and any career working in the great outdoors.

*Me trying to chase down Yorktown All-American midfielder, Rob Hoynes, in a 1981 high school game at Yorktown. Hoynes, a great guy, went on to play and earn All-American honors at the U.S. Military Academy at West Point. We played together down in the old Freeport league on Long Island and against each other in college.*

When I made the transition from junior to senior year in high school, the reality of graduation hit me. Sports was something I loved, and most sports came relatively easy to me. In high school, I earned All-County honors my senior year, which, considering the district I played in, was no small feat. However, I barely made a blip on the screens of college recruiters. I received two letters from Division III coaches and applied to those schools—the State University of New York at Cortland and Hobart Colleges—but failed to gain admission to either. When my mother talked to my guidance counselor about finding an appropriate school for me, the counselor suggested Herkimer County Community College (HCCC) in the Mohawk Valley, because high school teammates of mine had played lacrosse there the previous year.

*Yup, that's me in the front with hair, wearing number seven, and thinking I'm too cool for school in the spring of 1982. This was taken during my first year as a Herkimer General in front of the athletic department at Herkimer County Community College located in New York's Mohawk Valley between Albany and Syracuse.*

I enrolled at HCCC in the fall of 1981. At the end of the semester, the players from my high school lacrosse team had failed out of school, leaving me the last Crotonite. My many years as a college professor since then led me to think that they had not been ready to make the commitment necessary to succeed in college at the time. I've seen this happen on more than one occasion with students. College isn't for everyone. I would suggest that you not make an expensive investment in a college education until you know what your gift is. You are better off working together with professionals to find the right training space for your gift and for when you are ready to develop it. Get your gifts and talents assessed carefully. We'll talk more about this topic later in the chapter on getting the right training for your gift.

In 1988, I had been out of college for a little more than two and a half years. I was in my mid-twenties, single, living at home with my folks and paying rent to them, and working as a physical education teacher in the Danbury Public School system in Danbury, Connecticut. I needed a master's degree to meet the educational requirement to obtain tenure as a public schoolteacher, but I had no clue what to study in graduate school.

One day I saw a poster advertising a free, six-week evening career exploration course at a local public library in Westchester County. That was one of the best courses I have ever taken—and I have a high school degree, an associate's degree, a bachelor's degree, a master's degree, and a PhD! I also teach courses for a living, so I know a bit about teaching and content. My classmates in the course were mostly older than me; they seemed like people who either wanted or had to do what I have come to call *a career makeover*.

During the course, we took diagnostic tests and had discussions about our gifts, talents, and abilities. All indicators showed a strong direction toward teaching history. I had started reading the history books in my parents' home after my mother had given me the autobiography of my namesake, the abolitionist Frederick Douglass, who was born on the Eastern Shore of Maryland about three decades before the US Civil War.[8] I also read the autobiography of Malcolm X, who had also undertaken a self-directed education focusing on history.[9] By the time the course was over, it was clear that I should be teaching history at the college level.

*An 1862 portrait of my namesake, Frederick Douglass, courtesy of the Library of Congress.*

*Malcolm X, right, greeting Martin Luther King, 1964, courtesy of the Library of Congress*

The second most important course that helped me identify my gifts and talents was also free. As a graduate student, I joined a church that had an extensive new member orientation. In addition to learning the essential history of the church and the ABCs of the Christian faith, the last section of the orientation focused on understanding your spiritual gifts. I learned that God has given everyone a gift to serve for the greater good of society.

But for now I want to hammer home the point that you do have a gift, and, in most instances, more than one gift. Let me give you an illustration that will help clarify this point. I live about a ten-minute drive from work. When I need time to get away and knock out some writing I will go to my office on the weekend. Last week I packed up my computer, got in the car, and headed to the office. However, when I got there I reached into my pocket for the key to the building where my office is housed and I couldn't find it. I looked all over my car, in my computer bag, and in all my pockets. In frustration, I returned home. I continued to look for the key to get into the office the next day. It was frustrating because I'm very intentional about being organized, which means I put my keys in the same place so that I don't lose them. After looking around the house for about thirty minutes, I gave up and started getting ready for bed. As I was getting undressed, I took off a belt that holds my smartphone when I'm exercising. The belt has a pocket for the smartphone and a smaller pocket where I keep my driver's license and school ID. There I found my office key. I had the key the entire time but forgot where I put it.

I think you know where I'm going. Many of us have a gift from God but we don't know it, and we continue to wander through life trying to discover how to enter the right career door. You will never be able to enter the right career door without discovering the gifts that God has given you. Know now that you have gifts from God that he has given you to serve others. One of Zig Ziglar's many mantras is, "You can have everything in life you want, if you will just help other people get what they want."[10] Think about that. If you use your God-given gifts to help others, in the process you will get what you need, want, and desire. Too many people are like the little boy Jimmy who prayed to God, "Gimme gimme gimme; my name is Jimmy." What if Jimmy had prayed, "Lord, show me what my gift is and how to use it to meet the needs of others"?

It gives me tremendous joy when I have the opportunity to use my gift of teaching others. I teach professionally and I teach pro bono, and in both scenarios I get fired up because I love teaching. As I like to say, I have a vocation that feels more like a vacation. Don't get me wrong. Your gift doesn't mean you're going to travel down the road of life without ever needing a snowplow. No, the storms of life will come, but when you stay in the lane where God has gifted you, you will learn something valuable that will be a blessing to you and others, and you will be wiser for it.

## Passion, Talent, and Your Gift

Passion is an intense emotion, but it's not your gift. You will develop passion for your gift when you learn more about it and perfect it over time. Your gift is not your talent. Talent can be learned, but gifts are innate.[11] You can use your talents, but your gift will make a way for you and put you in the presence of great people (read Proverbs 22:29).

Your success will be related to the gift God has given you to serve others and how you choose to use it. It will open all the mysteries of your life—and make clear your mission in life. It will give your life new meaning and direction.

## Your Gift Mark

Steve Harvey says that using your gift with your personal skills and talents is your "gift mark"—that which sets you apart when you use your gift. It's what people come to expect when they hire you to do your thing.[12] People expect a well-packaged, informative, and inspiring word or lesson from me. They expect me to stay on message, speak succinctly, and keep to the schedule. People have also come to associate me with good-tasting food because they know I love to cook.

It's important to say here that we don't have control over the gifts that we have. We gain them as God distributes them to us. Requesting another gift if you think it's cooler than yours is only going to frustrate you (read Romans 11:29 and James 1:17).

When I transferred to SU to continue my education and athletic career as a lacrosse player, I learned just how underdeveloped in terms of fitness conditioning I was. But strength and conditioning coach Mike Woicik used to say to me that my upper body should sue my legs for lack of support. Translation: "You don't have well-developed leg muscles." It didn't become an excuse for me not to work hard in the gym doing squats, leg extensions, leg curls, or other lower-body exercises. I worked hard on my lower body. But I had to accept that no matter how hard I worked I wouldn't have the lower body of my teammate, Hall of Famer Brad Kotz. The same is true with your gift. The Bible tells us that our gift is from the Holy Spirit and it's distributed according to his will (read Hebrews 2:4). The sooner you accept that and move on, the better off you are going to be.

Our Creator's expectation is that you receive your gift and use it to serve others and use it faithfully (read 1 Peter 4:10). As I said earlier, unfortunately, I didn't learn what I'm sharing with you here until I was in my twenties. Why did it take so long? Because in part I was immature and hard-headed. And in part because I, like a lot of you, experienced some traumatic situations growing up that caused me to function like the soldier coming home from battle with PTSD who remains undiagnosed for months and sometimes years. As a child, my oldest brother, who had his own problems and died early because of them, sexually molested me, which in many ways short-circuited my ability to operate as a fully functioning child of God. Instead, I stumbled along as a wounded soldier trying to tough it out in life without treating the emotional wound that I had suffered as a child. I share this with you because if something similar has caused you a great deal of pain and you don't seek the necessary help, there's a good chance you're going to self-destruct and hurt others. I saw an *Oprah* show dedicated to the phenomena of men who, like me, had been molested as children. Her entire audience consisted of men who shared a similar childhood trauma as me. It made me realize that the sexual molesting of boys is more common than I had ever known. The saying is true that secrets lead to sickness and there are too many who have an emotional walking pneumonia and they need treatment just like I did.

I never talked about what happened to me until I was in my twenties and I hit a wall emotionally. I had to and I'm glad I did go get help in the form of intensive counseling and ongoing coaching. I am mindful of the importance of keeping myself healthy emotionally because of what happened. When someone acts out in a negative way that seems blown out of proportion and straight up nasty, I tell my children that hurt people hurt people. So, ask yourself, have I taken the steps necessary to heal the wounded child within me? Are people able to easily push my buttons, triggering me to say and do things that I regret when I calm down? Do I fly off the handle too often or self-medicate to make myself feel better with food, alcohol, sex, stealing, shopping, gambling, or pornography? If so, like me, you need help and you need it now.

I grew up in a home with two parents who did the best they could but they never got over traumatic situations in their own lives. My mother grew up in a home with a stepfather who had been an alcoholic and made her home life difficult to endure. Perhaps that explains why she later became so engaged as a community activist working to improve the lives of the marginalized. I don't know the whole story but what I can piece together as an historian, her stepfather made her feel marginalized in her own home. My mother had the amazing ability to engage people and make them feel like they were special and she had been a gifted public speaker. But she, like many of us, had issues. At home, she had a contentious relationship with my father, and the two of them would disrespect each other and speak to each other in ways that had not been good for me as a young kid growing up. As I got older, my mother and I constantly got into arguments and she would say things that would destroy the development of my self-confidence. She would tell others how proud she was of me but she found it difficult to say this to me directly.

My father had grown up in a home with a mother who did not shower him with love and affection, so he had a hard time doing that with his own children. As many of my high school friends said, "Your dad wasn't a man to play with," and that's fairly accurate. As I said, they did the best they could, but because my parents never dealt with their own childhood issues and lacked a clear vision of their gifts, they had limitations on how much they could help me.

Here are 3 Ps that will help you better understand what you are passionate about and thereby recognize your gift. I have also provided questions and examples from the experience of individuals using their gifts that will help you identify yours. What do you enjoy reading? What do you consider the perfect gift for you? What do you create and emulate? What do you dream about and have visions of doing?

Artist Sachiko Akiyama recalls that when she was in kindergarten she remembers seeing Scotch tape for the first time. "It was around Christmas time, and I asked my parents to buy me a roll. They thought that I wanted it to wrap presents. Instead I took the tape and made a giant ball out of it. And I've been making art out of all kinds of materials ever since." Babson College Chief of Police Jim Pollard says: "As young as age six, I had a passion for reading crime-solving Detective Dick Tracy comic books. Sikh broadcaster Harnarayan Singh was raised in Alberta, Canada. As a young child, he exhibited a love of ice hockey and the gifts of a broadcaster emulating play-by-play announcers he heard calling games on television. "My family realized that I was interested in the announcing side of it, so they proceeded to give me this toy microphone and a stand from RadioShack. And that for me was just the perfect toy."[13]

Ask those who know you best what they see as your gifts. Don't be surprised if they have a consensus opinion about them. What are the topics you could talk about for hours and do? Having a mentor who can help you identify your gifts or who has the same or a similar gift is critically important to making over your life for good. That's what we turn to in the next chapter: the importance of having a mentor.

# CHAPTER 2

# Get a Mentor

The first ingredient in the recipe I'm sharing with you is understanding that you have a gift. The second ingredient to understand, monetize, and serve others with your gift is you must have mentors. We all need mentors who can help us understand our gift and how to develop it into a blessing. In this chapter I provide examples of mentors in my life, on and off the field. I use these short anecdotes in part as the memoir aspect of this book but also as a teaching tool to show you examples of similar mentors you could seek out for yourself.

*Behind every person who gains some degree of recognition in their chosen endeavor, there is a Steve Mabus.*

### Steve Mabus

Steve Mabus was a timely mentor in my life. I started playing lacrosse in eighth grade, and the summer before I entered high school Steve Mabus moved to a house three hundred yards from my family home on Batten Road in the village of Croton-on-Hudson. Steve played college lacrosse at Kutztown State in Pennsylvania. I don't remember how it started, but before I knew it, Steve and I started playing catch, shooting on goal, and playing one-on-one in his yard. He poured so much into me, a skinny kid whom he patiently taught everything he had learned in college up until that time. Steve played in a college summer league at the Lakeland Middle School field twenty minutes north of Croton, and he started taking me along to his games. It was an amazing experience for me as a young player. I remember watching Scott Finlay (West Point Military Academy), Scott Nelson (North Carolina State University), Bill Simunek (St. Lawrence University), Greg Rivers (University of Delaware), and Clay Johnson (University of Maryland) play. These guys were terrific athletes with great sticks and lacrosse IQ. Watching them provided a visual image of how the game should be played.

## The God Squad

Spiritually, I had a group of mentors off the field during my undergraduate days at SU. At the beginning of the spring 1984 semester, I came to faith in Jesus Christ and became a regular at Paul and Sandy Jewel's Friday night Campus Bible Fellowship. Over time, I became a member of the "God Squad" (SU football players Rodney Carter, Vic Bellamy, Bernard King, and Glen Moore), as the student athletes called us.

*Bernard King, former SU and Canadian Football League Linebacker and Pastor of Cornerstone Bible Fellowship in Florida*

Most of us at the fellowship were student athletes who wanted to study the Bible, pray, and grow in a relationship with Jesus Christ. On reflection, I patterned how I carried myself after them because I saw that people respected them. I grew to hold their friendship in high regard. I don't know what my coaches or teammates made out of so much change in my life; I stopped going to the team parties and did not see teammates much off the field. I enjoyed competing with my teammates on the field and liked them, but I spent my time off the field with members of the God Squad. I got along with my teammates but I no longer sought their social acceptance and the game of lacrosse no longer served as an addiction for me as it had grown to be after I started playing in eighth grade.

I want you to think about what I just said: Are you addicted to the sport that you play? Or perhaps you're addicted to winning? If you don't win, are you absolutely miserable to be around or are you unable to sleep at night because of the loss? You're not just competitive, you're addicted to sports and/or winning. I've seen this phenomenon with sports fans—folks who aren't even playing in the game but their response is similar to athletes when they lose. If that's the case you're addicted, and, no joke, I suggest you do something about it and get some help quick. Anything that has too much control over your mood and emotions is a straight up addiction. I know of people who have allowed the people they are dating to have that kind of control over their life. It's not healthy, and is not normal, so don't think it is and get some help.

## Mike Woicik

In addition to the members of the God Squad, SU strength and conditioning coach Mike Woicik served as another important friend and mentor. Members of the God Squad introduced me to Mike; they had become tight from so much time spent together in the weight room. Mike would later write the book *Total Conditioning for Football: The Syracuse Way* and go on to hold the record for Super Bowl rings for an NFL coach: three with the Dallas Cowboys and three with the New England Patriots. Mike and Patriots head coach Bill Belichick share this record.[14]

As a result of the God Squad, I became a convert to Christianity and strength training. Through Mike, that year I became a fan of lifting weights and of the Philadelphia sound of Blue Magic. Mike wrote a program designed to strengthen my legs and upper body, with his mantra being, "Upper body for show [to show off], legs to go [power and speed]!" I became a Woicik disciple and worked out four days per week: lower body Monday, upper body Tuesday, Wednesday off, the same routine Thursday and Friday, weekends off. I still do a modified version of that workout. No matter how well you know and understand the gift that God is giving you, you still need a mentor to show you how to develop it and use it wisely to serve others and make an income.

*Left to right: former SU, New England Patriots, and currently Dallas Cowboys strength coach Mike Woicik—6 Super Bowl rings, former SU and Cowboys fullback, NFL analyst Daryl Johnston—3 Super Bowl rings, and former SU running back coach Jim Hofher*

## Mike McTighe

Gettysburg College Professor of Religion Mike McTighe served as an important mentor in my life after I made the decision to become a college professor, researcher, and writer. By example, he showed me what it meant to make a commitment to become a college professor, he answered my questions, and he demonstrated his confidence in my intellectual ability by asking me to co-teach my first college course with him. In addition, he offered to write letters of support for my application to PhD programs. Shortly after the course started, Mike told me that doctors had diagnosed him with cancer. He asked me to continue teaching the course alone and assured me that I could handle it. I completed the semester teaching without Mike. He later succumbed to the cancer. I will never forget the guidance and support he provided for me early in my career.

## Sarah Hughes

During the fall of 1990, my second year of the Shippensburg University (Ship) master's degree in history program, I met Sarah Hughes, who served as another important mentor in my life. She joined the history faculty at Ship when I needed to select an advisor for my senior thesis. She would have me come to her house after class and discuss books that she would give me to read. She later told me that she used the book discussions as a way of testing my commitment to the study of history.

At the time, I worked at Gettysburg College as a graduate assistant in the athletic department, helping to coach lacrosse and soccer. I also had a job as an assistant to the dean of a department on campus. My plan was to gain admission to a PhD program in history with full funding after the completion of my master's degree in history. However, shortly before I started the application process, Gettysburg College Treasurer and Business Manager Bill VanArsdale (Van) offered me the opportunity to serve as an interim dean. At Syracuse University I competed against his son, Mark, who played lacrosse at Hobart College. Syracuse and Hobart have had a long-standing but friendly rivalry in lacrosse and Van knew me from my playing days and how I conducted myself on the field. During the meeting in which he offered me the position, he told me that he had done so because he had been watching me as I went about doing my job as a graduate assistant at Gettysburg and he liked the work ethic I showed. Somebody is always watching even when you don't know it. Do the right thing because it is the right thing to do and doing the right thing consistently will open doors of opportunity for you in the long run and when you least expect it. Integrity is who you are when nobody else is watching. It had been my integrity and God's grace that put me in position to receive the job offer from Van.

I was twenty-nine years old when I received Van's unexpected offer. I went to Professor Hughes and asked her advice: Should I turn the opportunity down and enter a PhD program or take a year off from graduate school to serve as an interim dean? Professor Hughes told me that at my age the opportunity to be an interim dean would be a game-changer in my career and that I should take the time off from graduate school and do it. I did just what she said and it has made a great difference in the opportunities I've had since then. The position gave me not only the essential experience that shaped my decision to continue on the track of a teacher, coach, and researcher but an income that allowed me to pay off my remaining undergraduate student loans, make the transportation and clothing upgrades I needed, and save money for graduate school.

## Dr. Otey M. Scruggs

Syracuse University Professor of History Otey M. Scruggs became another important mentor for me during my graduate school years. I was about to complete the master's program in history at Shippensburg, where I had written a master's thesis on the abolitionist movement. Professor Scruggs had written in that area, which led me to apply to the PhD program in history at Syracuse. I contacted him to try to find out if he could serve as my dissertation advisor.[15] In many ways, I'd vetted him like a person applying for acceptance to the Secret Service training program. He was impressed with my diligence and we hit it off on the phone.

*Dr. Otey M. Scruggs*

Professor Scruggs had earned a PhD in history from Harvard University in 1958. Before the 1970s, very few African Americans had degrees from Ivy League schools nevermind doctorate degrees. We had similar backgrounds in athletics; he was a decathlete at the University of California at Santa Barbara. In fact, he received an invitation to the US Olympic Trials, losing a spot on the team to the gold medalist Rafer Johnson. Professor Scruggs advocated for me and got the Dean's Office at the Maxwell School to see that I gained a tuition scholarship. This happened after the history department had already given out scholarship money to its incoming class of graduate students. This was a real break for me because I did not get accepted to any other graduate programs.

Professor Scruggs also kept me from making a poor decision toward the end of my PhD program. I started getting tired of being a poor graduate student and prematurely considered entering the job market. I saw numerous jobs posted and I had been itching to make some money. I called him and asked him what he thought. He gently but firmly advised me not to do it. His rationale was that when you take a tenure track position teaching history at a college or university, time preparing for class and grading, attending faculty meetings, and meeting service requirements means little to no time to finish writing one's dissertation. I took his advice and took myself off the job market. I've been a college professor for sixteen years at the time of writing this book. With the experience I now have, I realize that going into the job market before I finished my studies would have been a mistake. Thank God for mentors!

## Why Is a Mentor Important?

Mentors serve as counselors, guides, tutors, and coaches. They can open doors for you to gain important work experience and skills. They can provide passports to spaces and people such as decision and policy makers. Mentors can answer questions based on their experience and 50,000-foot perspective. They have a wealth of experience that can help you make good choices in your field of interest. An experienced mentor can advise you on the type of job experiences that will profit you the most, suggest projects you should undertake, and help you reflect on your job experience. They can also serve as important mediators when you run into a rough patch and need to make significant career decisions.[16]

Ask your mentor for suggested reading in the field in which you're interested. Ask your mentor about their career and their journey in getting where they are today. A question I like to ask people doing something I want to do is, if they were starting over again, what route they would take to get where they are today?[17] Shadow your mentor for a day to better understand their job responsibilities. On a regular basis, discuss your thoughts and experiences with your mentor and ask for their feedback. If you're thinking about one thing over another, ask your mentor what they think. Before making a pitch to a higher-up, run it by your mentor first to determine the merit of what you're considering saying and/or doing.[18]

A mentor is an experienced and trusted advisor who can help us reach our goals. They help keep us focused and provide an excellent sounding board for us to bounce our ideas off before we plunge into them. They'll keep us off the rabbit trail and on the most direct route to achieving our desired result. It's great to have a mentor in your organization who has the 50,000-foot view. They are in a key position to learn about opportunities in your area of interest. They can let other people in your field know about your skills and abilities and recommend you for job openings that others are trying to fill. Are there people whose work and or career you admire? If so, consider approaching them, and do so tactfully so that you don't get on their nerves.[19]

## Choosing a Mentor

Choose a mentor who has climbed the mountain that you're interested in climbing. Someone who has years of experience and has been proven to be battle-tested is far better in your corner than a newbie. That person will be well-networked and well-suited to give you advice. They'll possess a certain wisdom that comes only from lived experience and making—and learning from—lots of mistakes.[20]

Be sure to select a mentor whom you respect and admire—and one who is accessible. When you get to know such a person, you have nothing to lose by approaching them and asking if they would consider serving as your mentor. If they say no, then don't push the issue. You want somebody who is willing and able. Compared with a friend or family member, a mentor can provide impartial advice, rooted in knowledge and experience. They also have access to other sources of advice, guidance, and assistance that you do not have.[21]

When looking for a mentor, focus on people who possess the qualities and networks that will help you advance. You want people who have an excellent track record of success in the areas in which you're trying to gain traction. Mentors can provide important introductions and help you negotiate new circumstances, as well as increase your visibility by your association with them. The best of them give great constructive criticism in the form of a sandwich: good news, bad news, ending with good news. Here are three tips for how to approach someone about becoming your mentor:

1. Develop some regular interactions with them first to determine if it's a good fit
2. Put your best foot forward
3. Approach them like a prospective employer
4. Do your homework about them

Inquire if this potential mentor has time in their life and career to mentor you. A great mentor is someone who is available and not just knowledgeable. You want someone who enjoys the process of coaching others. Some people are talented, but it doesn't make them great coaches. You want a mentor who is a great teacher.[22] Here are some keys to a successful mentoring experience from Dave Ramsey, host of *The Dave Ramsey Show*. On a daily basis, I listen to about three hours of his podcast. He has gotten more people out of debt than anybody else in the country and he provides sound career advice. Here are three suggestions he shares about mentors:

1. **Choose wisely:** The goal of this relationship is to make your habits and values better as you become like the people you spend time with. Your mentor can be someone you know personally or someone you've never met as long as you learn valuable lessons from their example.
2. **Take action:** Follow through and act on what you've learned.
3. **Change it up:** You will need different types of mentors for different areas and phases in your life.[23]

## Conclusion

A mentor is someone who has been battled-tested and is willing to share the lessons they have learned with us. Mentors help us understand why we need specific training, steps, and habits to successfully serve others with our gift and make an income. Our mentor should be someone from whom we can receive. The person who would be a great mentor for you would not necessarily be a great mentor for someone else. What works best for you in terms of a mentor's gender, age, cultural disposition? I know folks who, because of their cultural baggage, find it difficult to receive from white males with southern accents like Dave Ramsey. The stereotype of a white Southerner makes it too hard for them to hear their sound advice. I'm just keeping it real. The same is true if you grew up as a white Southerner and in a home or community that has held people of African American heritage like me in contempt. Some men have been raised with contempt for women, so having a female mentor is problematic. By the way, I would not suggest that you get a mentor of the opposite gender for whom a sexual attraction could develop despite an age difference of ten years or more. Need I say more? Take all these things into consideration as you consider approaching someone to be your mentor or if someone comes to you to mentor them.

# CHAPTER 3

# Choose the Right School and Training

Although I have a PhD, I'm not convinced that college is the best choice for preparing someone to use their gift to serve others and make a good income. Why? Because the best match for your gift should determine the work in which you start using it. As I will say many times throughout this book, I liken the work you do as a type of vehicle you drive to get you from point A to point B. That's what a job is for me, a vehicle that I use to serve others and make an income in the process. It's essential for you to have mentors who understand the type of training you will need to best fit your gift to the type of vehicles you will be using it in over the next five to ten years.

Once you've done that assessment and received mentoring, you're ready to start the training process. A great mentor would know the type of training you will need to serve others and make a good income. There are too many people who enroll in schools and training without first doing step one—identifying their gift and then assessing the best vehicles for it with an experienced professional. How do I know this? Because I have met them as students who enroll in the classes that I have taught over the last several decades.

I know people who are undereducated for their vocation and folks who are overeducated for their vocation, and in most cases this happened because they didn't understand their gift and they didn't seek or have access to great mentors. The key is an affordable school or training program that you can cash-flow. And despite what everybody around you is going to tell you, you don't need to take out student loans to get yourself ready to use your gift.

Second, there are lots of vocations in which an apprenticeship and on-the-job experience are the best training, making formal education and a degree program unnecessary, if not overkill. I have met professionals who have taken the apprenticeship and job experience route and they are tops in their field. The one I'm thinking about now has a good-sized staff with lots of employees with undergraduate and graduate degrees working under his supervision. Think about that—you have the college degrees and the student loans to show for them, and the person you report to has none of them, nor the debt!

What's been happening over the last twenty-five years or more is that we show favoritism. That is, we value and privilege the college-educated and the work they do over the non-college-educated and vocationally educated and the work *they* do. The Bible tells us not to do this because, in the process, you're going to overlook someone God has gifted and sent to serve you, meet your needs, and add to your collective benefit. We see a similar favoritism in scripture based on one's height, weight, and wealth that we are warned to heed (see Samuel 16:1-13 and James 2:1-4).

You have to have the conviction that God has gifted you with something you can do that nobody else can do, and it's up to you to get the training to do it to the best of your ability so you can serve those around you and make a great income. You also have to find a mentor who understands this and doesn't favor the vocationally trained over the college-trained or vice versa.

There must've been a lot of people praying for me when I was an adolescent. Because like so many young athletes, when I went to college, I did so to continue my playing career, and that's the truth, as pitiful as it is. I find that to be the case for many of the outstanding athletes I've had an opportunity to interview on my podcast. That's about as deep as most of us are as adolescents with undeveloped executive functioning in the frontal cortex of our brains. This is the part of the brain responsible for analyzing, deciding, and making long-term decisions with their consequences in mind.[24]

As an adult with a fully functioning frontal cortex, I am convinced that the key to success is knowing what your weaknesses are. Until we are in our late twenties, the majority of us do not have the capacity to make decisions by considering the long-term consequences—decisions such as what's the best way for me to be prepared and trained to use my gift to serve others and make a great income. We need mentors who can help us make important decisions that will have long-term consequences, people who can speak into our lives without clouded judgment.[25]

A mentor can help you see down the road, prepare you for the bumps ahead, and show you how to avoid the ditches and obstacles that are around the corner. It sure is comforting to know that somebody has driven the road you're heading down and knows what's to come. It doesn't mean that your drive will be easy. A great mentor is like having an American Automobile Association (AAA) membership card in your wallet. AAA provides an 800 number on the card I keep in my wallet. I call them anytime I run into a problem on the road, including when my battery goes dead or I get a flat tire because of a pothole. I can tell you from experience that potholes in ditches can damage your vehicle and the experience can be humiliating, particularly when you end up in a bad place because you tried to make a decision on your own, being too hardheaded to pick up the phone and ask for help before you choose between two or more routes to get prepared to use your gift.

Landing in a ditch straight up sucks, wastes time, and it's expensive. Those of us who are hardheaded think we can get out on our own, and we end up messing up the car even more in the process. Learn how to depend on somebody wiser and smarter to help you avoid the ditches and to get you out of those you end up in. A good mentor can keep you from paying the stupid tax that is levied on your life when you try to make important decisions about training without the aid of a fully functioning frontal cortex. Do you want to make an important decision about how to prepare to use your gift to make a living and make a difference in this world with a faulty decision-maker? Or would it be better to make that same choice with the help of mentors with track records of excellent long-term planning and wise decisions? Pardon the pun, but it seems like a no-brainer to me.

I didn't have the advantage of reading this chapter before choosing the best place to prepare me to use my gift. If you still want an excuse for making a dumb decision about being prepared to use your gift, then you should stop reading now. I'm about to pull the blinders from your eyes about how to become prepared and fully functional to use your gift to serve others and meet your financial responsibilities.

## The Every-Child-Needs-to-Go-to-College Myth

In North America, we started preaching that every child needs to go to college. The notion is well-meaning but narrow-minded, and the idea has had the negative result of devaluing and dishonoring occupations that don't require a four-year college degree and the people who perform them. The everybody-needs-to-go-to-college sermon has contributed to a student loan crisis that has hamstrung the wealth-building potential of millions of citizens. Too many people who have gone to college in this country have done so without a clear and well-thought-out reason for why they needed a degree and how it would allow them to better use their gift to make an income and serve others. Without that compelling *why*, a student lacks the focus necessary in most instances to excel in school and complete their studies as soon as possible. The compelling reason inspires us to give our best effort to be prepared to serve others with our gift in the most cost-effective way possible. This is the dilemma that I see regularly as a college professor: "I'm so glad to be here but I have no clue what I'm going to do after I graduate, *if* I graduate. I had the goal of getting accepted here, but now that I'm here, I'm confused about how I'm going to monetize what I'm learning. I feel like a wandering generality because I see no connection between what's on the inside of me that I'm gifted to do and love to do, and my courses, major, and minor."

The everyone-needs-to-go-to-college sermon has resulted in a labor shortage in the construction industry and others sectors in our economy for great-paying jobs that have often gone under the radar because we were so focused on kids going to college. This section of the book is my attempt at a cultural change in North America. We need to revise the message delivered to adolescents in their homes, communities, churches, synagogues, mosques, and schools. As it relates back to the chapter on identifying one's gift, adolescents, get the training and development necessary for your gift to flourish! Second, the laborer is worthy of hiring. With a shoutout to the mission of former *Dirty Jobs* television host Mike Rowe, all work is honorable. Get the knowledge you need to exercise your gift and make an impact on the world around you, and do so without going into debt!

Regularly, people in their twenties and early thirties will say to me that they want to get a graduate degree and want my advice. When I inquire why, I learn that they *feel* it's essential for them to use their gift in a specific career. More often than not, they are seeking degrees because they are insecure. **College degrees don't end feelings of insecurity**. I encourage you to seek the help necessary to address the insecurity that's gnawing away at your soul.

## Training for Vocational Jobs

There's a serious shortage today of people gifted to work with their hands as electricians, plumbers, carpenters, welders, and other trades. These jobs require vocational training and apprenticeships. One can prepare to perform these jobs in some cases in as little as three to six months of intensive vocational training that, on average, costs around $6,000 per student. The cost for a public four-year college degree is approximately $32,800 per student.[26]

But beware of schools and advertising that offer fast results to begin one's career and earn great wages while in school. There is no quick route to a great-paying job. Programs that appear quick and lucrative are more often than not get-rich-quick schemes that exploit naïve or greedy people. Students who start such programs rarely complete them and drop out with enormous amounts of debt that still must be paid back. Beware of being talked into committing to an occupation you know little about because some advertisement is promising lucrative wages for little work. You know you're about to be ripped off when you ask about the program requirements and one or more of the following is shared with you: that you must pay a fee to hold a space for you, pay back loans prior to completing the program, and pay to take extra licensing exams after the coursework is completed. The wise person gets better and more affordable training at an accredited community college. However, before registering for any program after graduating from high school, learn what your gift is and—then and only then—commit to a career that's the right fit for you. Research shows that youth who attend for-profit schools have had terrible experiences and have not improved their earning potential based on the training they received. The outcomes can best be described as horrendous.[27]

Here are some tips for acquiring affordable vocational training:

1. The best short-term training programs have strong partnerships with employers, trainers, and program coordinators.
2. Private institutions and programs are typically four times more expensive than public ones. Therefore, go the public school route, so long as the program you're entering has a track record of helping people get prepared for their vocation.
3. The best programs have statistics on the average income of its graduates over at least ten years. If it doesn't, it's a suspect program and you should stay away from it.

## Kevin DeSantis

I grew up playing hockey with Kevin DeSantis who was the second born of three boys. Both his parents had college degrees and so did the parents of most of his friends who he went to school with him in Scarsdale, New York, which is a wealthy suburb of New York City. His mother was a stay-at-home mom. His father had been an executive in the cosmetics industry who wore a white dress shirt, tie, dark suit, and he commuted into New York City on the train like so many parents that Kevin knew who held white-collar jobs.

Kevin like most of his classmates heard the sermon go to college; and that's what the majority of the graduates of prestigious Scarsdale High School have done. Kevin had been an exceptional hockey player and he wanted to continue playing hockey after high school. However, like me, his athletic and academic achievements did not put him on the radar of college admissions directors or coaches. With Kevin's buy-in, his parents enrolled him into a prestigious New England boarding school as a postgraduate—students who do another year of high school to improve their academic and, in many instances, athletic performance. The school has an outstanding ice hockey program; alumni gain admissions to outstanding collegiate hockey programs and later professional careers in the NHL. Kevin played well enough at the boarding school to attract the attention of some college coaches but not good enough to earn an athletic scholarship.

But as early as middle school Kevin had been aware of his gift for repairing and building things although he had done little to develop it until his last years of high school. The father of a neighborhood friend ran a business installing and repairing furnaces. Kevin and his friend worked within the business when they could to make spending money. Kevin learned that he had a natural ability to understand and perform the work. He also liked the opportunity the work gave him to explore different parts of metropolitan New York such as Yonkers, New Rochelle, and the Bronx and meet all kinds of people. Kevin later had the opportunity to work with his uncle who built houses for a living during long boarding school breaks. He says working with his uncle showed him that he also had a propensity and enjoyment for carpentry.

But Kevin had a problem. People in his family, community, and school expected him to go to college. In the absence of college coaches aggressively seeking to recruit him to come and play hockey, Kevin returned to Scarsdale and enrolled in a college engineering program figuring that would be a good fit for somebody like him who had a talent for working with his hands. He continued to work in the furnace and homebuilding industries to make money and in the process he learned more and got better at them.

Kevin relocated to sunny southern California and enrolled in classes at UCLA to complete his engineering degree. To pay the bills, he worked in the building trades. Before long, he had his own crew and a successful business as a residential and commercial builder. Kevin has yet to complete the coursework for an engineering degree, something which he regrets. But he has finally embraced his gift that has given him a thriving business in the building industry that employs a crew and subcontractors with crews. While in the process of writing this book, Kevin and I had long phone calls about his journey to discovering his gift and the frustration that he has seen from other people from similar backgrounds who have not yet understood and monetized their gift. Most recently he said that he cannot find enough US citizens to work on his crew doing hard work for good wages, and recent executive orders on immigration have sent foreign-born workers packing or into hiding. It's really sad to see people who are frustrated because they have not discovered and developed their gift. And it's sad seeing good-paying jobs in the building trades not be filled. I will say it again and I'll keep saying it until people hear me—a college education is not for everyone.

## College and University Training

In my case, I got a PhD because it's a job requirement in my field: no PhD, no job serving students as a college professor and receiving a good income for doing so. Now, staying with the college professor case study, the key to training is choosing an affordable school to get what you need. Most folks go into debt to pay for the education they need but can't afford. Others go into debt because, instead of paying for what they need and can afford, they take out loans for what they want or desire. Other folks obtain more education than they need and thereby waste unnecessary time. Get the training you need, in a timely fashion, and pay cash for it. People care more about your ability to do your job than where you received your training. I have met folks who are recognized experts in their field and earn a great income who have Ivy League degrees, state school degrees, and no degrees. I suspect you are like me—you don't ask the healthcare professionals who keep you feeling good or the pilots who successfully take you from one airport to the next where they went to school and or did their training.

If your training calls for a degree, make sure you're getting the right degree. Do you need an associate's (two years), bachelor's (four years), master's (a four-year undergraduate degree plus an additional one or two years), law (a four-year undergraduate degree plus an additional two or three years), or doctorate (a four-year undergraduate degree plus an additional five to seven years)? Count the cost in terms of time and money before you step into the classroom. Do you have the patience to be in school for the time necessary to complete the degree requirements? Are you seeking a degree that's going to require more money than you can cash-flow (pay for it in cash)? Completing a college degree program, whether it's a college, university, or a vocational program, is similar to running a race. It's more about endurance and perseverance than intelligence. You need to find out what the return on investment (ROI) is in the end. If it's not going to improve your ROI, then don't spend your time and money doing it, unless you just have plenty of extra time and money to use.

Here's what the research says about your earning potential based on your training, and keep in mind that there are exceptions to these points. First, the median lifetime earnings for bachelor's degree holders are highest in the following fields: management, health professional, science, technology, engineering, and mathematics—the so-called STEM (science, technology, engineering, and math) careers. The lowest-paying careers are in health support, education, and the service sector. Those from the STEM fields on average earned about $3 million compared to $1.2 million in non-STEM occupations.[28]

Second, you get the most out of college when you have substantial abstract thinking skills—the ability to calculate, sort, categorize, conceptualize, draw conclusions, interpret, and condense complex ideas. Also, the ability to adapt, be flexible, and use concepts and generalizations are all examples of abstract thinking. These skills develop between the ages of twelve and fifteen. They are absolutely necessary for succeeding in college.

Third, studies show that students don't necessarily develop a ton of new skills while in college. However, the completion of a college degree is an important signal to a potential employer that one has well-developed and necessary abstract thinking skills to perform and excel in a particular occupation or career. It is important for those selecting a college education to understand that an employer is paying for your ability to demonstrate a specific skill or perform a task and not for the name on your college degree. It's clear that job recruiters look at grades, majors, standardized test results, and the name of the school from which you graduated. It's also clear that graduates with STEM degrees have the highest estimated average lifetime earnings. Studies also show that, on average, college graduates tend to enjoy a higher quality of life then non-graduates.[29]

## College Tuition and Fees

Recent statistics show that the annual tuition and fees for public four-year colleges are approximately $8,200 per year for in-state students and $20,770 for out-of-state students. The average cost for an undergraduate degree at a private institution is $28,500. An average student attending an in-state, public four-year college or university paid $2,490 in tuition and fees when grant aid and federal education tax credits and deductions had been added. Workers with only a high school diploma earned $32,000 a year on average and a student with a bachelor's degree earned approximately $56,000 per year or 75 percent more per year than the high school graduate. Research shows that the college decision should be based on the planned major, the long-term occupational goal, the likelihood of completing a degree program, and the affordability of the institution. Can you graduate from the school with no debt?[30]

One study shows that a two-year community college degree is a better investment than going directly into a public or private undergraduate degree program. You can get more bang for your buck earning an associate's degree and then transferring into a public four-year institution to complete your undergraduate degree. I also recommend community colleges for students who did not excel in high school or for students returning to school with study skills that are rusty.[31]

Research on the quality of teaching has shown that it's the same at a community college as a public or private four-year college or university. You're saving money and losing nothing in terms of the quality of the education. **In most cases, how hard you study is more important than where you study.** Research done in 2012 shows that, on average, an associate's degree would cost between $7,000 and $8,000, and a three-year registered nursing degree about $10,000.[32] That's less than half of what one would pay at a public university for the same degree. This tells us that a community college is approximately 36 percent less expensive than a four-year public university or college for the same tuition and fees. And it's even cheaper than the equivalent content at a private college and university.[33]

I attended Herkimer County Community College in my home state of New York where I got a great education and had an opportunity to continue playing sports. After two years, I had the opportunity to transfer to one of several good universities. I choose Syracuse University, where I obtained an undergraduate degree at one-fourth the cost because I went the community college route. In this country, community colleges do not hold the same status as four-year universities. Do you want a status symbol or a debt-free education that allows you to begin using your gift to serve others and make an income?

Private institutions' tuition and fees are generally higher per student than those at public institutions. Publicly funded institutions frequently charge higher tuition for out-of-state students. In addition, they give admission priorities to students from their states. As a result, out-of-state students pay a premium to attend a publicly funded university in a state other than their own. In many cases, the increases are comparable to private college tuition rates. However, some states have reciprocal in-state agreements with neighboring states—for example, the bordering states of Wisconsin and Minnesota—so check the reciprocal agreements at the publicly funded universities where you live.[34] If you are a resident of Washington, DC, you are eligible for in-state tuition at all US state universities. That's awesome! That means residents of Washington, DC, can attend some of the best universities in the country. The University of Virginia; University of California at Berkeley the University of California at Los Angeles (UCLA); the University of Wisconsin-Madison; Florida State University; Ohio State University; and Pennsylvania State University are just a few of some of the best publicly funded universities in the country. But it's important to know if they have majors that will help develop your gift.

Private institutions can provide more financial aid to students than public institutions. Private institutions also tend to give aid to students in the form of grants, scholarships, and loans, and these grants offset the generally higher tuition rates that one pays for private colleges. Therefore, it is not uncommon for well-endowed private institutions to provide a more affordable or comparable cost to that of a publicly funded institution. Some public institutions will guarantee low-income students financial aid to graduate debt-free or with a minimum of student loan debt.[35]

In 2013, I had a postdoctoral fellowship at Harvard University. The fellowship came with work-study students to assist me with my research project. In the process of getting to know the students working with me that year, I asked each of them why they decided to come to Harvard. One student's answer is important to share here. She was a first generation college student from the state of Tennessee. She had the opportunity to attend a private school in Tennessee, most likely receiving financial aid at that school. But another student from her high school had come to Harvard before her and shared with her that Harvard gave them the best financial aid package out of all the schools to which she had applied and sought financial aid, making it affordable for her to attend such a prestigious university. The student working with me decided, therefore, to apply to Harvard. She had the grades to get accepted, and Harvard again provided and made a financial aid offer that made it a no-brainer for her to come.

The following year, a family friend had a son whom the Harvard football coaching staff had been recruiting. Ivy League institutions cannot offer athletic scholarships, but his family's financial need had been significant. The student athlete in question had an impeccable high school transcript that easily got him accepted to Harvard. And Harvard's financial aid office provided a financial aid package that enabled his single parent to send their child there for almost no money for all four years of his Harvard education. The moral of the story is: be aware of the price tag of the school you're looking at, but don't rule out the school until you see the financial support they can offer. Embrace grants and scholarships and refuse loans.

## Tips for Choosing a School

When deciding on a college, it pays to focus on schools that pass three important tests:

1.  Choose an institution with a track record of graduating its students in a timely manner. If it's a four-year institution, then you want to look at the school's six-year graduation track record. You can find that information on the website collegeresults.org. On average, that's what it takes most students to finish their undergraduate degrees.[36]
2.  Ideally, you want a college with an average class size of twenty students. You can find that information on the website collegedata.com.
3.  You want a place that's the right fit for you, and the only way to figure that out is to visit the campus and, if possible, attend classes. Speak to current students and alumni. If you want to be a student athlete, speak to the school's student athletes.

Alumni statistics are revealing in terms of job and earnings. *Money* magazine publishes the average annual salary within five years of graduation for the alumni of every college and rankings, so check out its website. The new federal college scorecard (collegescorecard.ed.gov) also reports the average 2011 earnings of all federal financial aid recipients who started as freshmen in each college in 2001. These two websites are gold mines for deciphering what your return on investment will be for a particular institution.

Save a good chunk of money by living at home instead of on campus. It is certainly true that when you live on campus you learn important skills, such as how to get along with people from different backgrounds and cultures and how to develop your social intelligence and empathy. However, I suggest you prioritize getting out of school without debt over these skills, which you can learn after you move out of your parents' home and get a roommate in your first apartment. I have observed as a professor that students who live off-campus are paying most often for a lifestyle choice where rent and food cost more than at home or in a dorm with a school cafeteria.

If you treat looking for scholarships as a job, dedicating a couple hours per week to it, you can get a good percentage of your schooling covered. Pursuing an athletic scholarship is like pursuing fool's gold, rocks that look like gold but have no value. You would do a lot better to take an SAT or ACT exam preparation course. If you score high on a standardized test, you will have colleges begging you to allow them to pay for your education.

I also suggest investing in a tax-free college savings plan, such as an educational savings account (ESA) or a 529 plan. What's the difference between them? The ESA has a limit of $2,000 per child every five years and has the benefit of allowing parents to invest in the type of growth stock mutual funds they like. ESAs are limited to families with less than a $200,000 household income. If they make more than that they must use a 529 plan, which is a state-specific plan that grows tax-free and gives parents the flexibility to contribute more than $2,000 per child. They can pick the type of 529 plan that allows them to choose the growth stock mutual funds they want. These plans can be transferred from one sibling to another in the case that one child decides not to go to college or earns a college scholarship that will cover all of their educational costs. You can withdraw and refund the amount of the scholarship a child earns without penalty or taxes. Be sure to check with a tax specialist before they acting.[37]

If you start early, either of these two plans will give you the ability to cash-flow a college education using growth stock mutual funds. And, in the process, you will enjoy life a whole lot better instead of spending every weekend traveling around the country to these athletic tournaments and college showcases. Folks, we need to wake up to the fact that youth sports have become a business in this country. There are club coaches promising athletic scholarships to those who play for their program, and that's just not the case in most instances. It's like the person who pays $10 a week to play the lottery and has been doing so for sixteen years. If they took $10 a week and invested it in a growth stock mutual fund at a minimum of 10 percent for the same amount of time, they would have more than enough to pay cash for your education after high school and a nice car to drive you back and forth from home to school during breaks!

Finally, work while you're in the training season of life. I worked while I went to school and played a varsity sport. I have observed as a professor that the students who work their way through college are more focused on how they spend their time (in class, out of class studying, and so on), and this work helps them excel as students. In graduate school, I worked as a teaching assistant, teaching small breakout groups in a large class and grading papers for the professor who taught the course. In exchange, I went to school tuition-free, had health benefits, and received a stipend for my living expenses and books. In addition to that teaching assistantship, I worked another ten hours or so per week at Dick's Sporting Goods. This was before Dick's had supersized stores across the country and their name on stadiums. In another instance, while doing several months of archival research in metropolitan Washington DC, I took a job at a food co-op. In exchange for the hours I worked, I received store credit to purchase groceries. Also, any of the edible products that got returned or damaged, I got to eat! That was one of my favorite jobs I had while in school. Another favorite job had been coaching at lacrosse camps. As a former Division I athlete from a signature program, I earned top dollar as a coach. What's my message? There are a lot of ways to cash-flow your education.

I haven't even mentioned yet the option of bartering your skills in exchange for free tuition, food, housing, and so on. While I was in school, I made ends meet in all kinds of ways, including purchasing most of my clothes at thrift shops, commuting to school by bike, and driving a car that didn't look good but ran well.

That's reminiscent of another strategy I had to make it through school. As a graduate student, I read the school paper's special events section, looked for events that included refreshments, attended them, and ate my fill. It worked particularly well when I studied late into the night off the energy I received from the food at those events. When I first started dating my wife she was in an MBA program full-time and I was a full-time PhD student. Many of our dates included walking the aisles at Whole Foods nibbling on the samples they had for customers! We still laugh about that strategy today. You can get through the schooling season of life without going into debt. You just have to be creative and persistent and learn how to live on a budget. Get the training you need instead of things you simply want if you don't have the cash to have both.

# CHAPTER 4

# Get an Internship

Five years ago, I had to replace my car. I purchased a car that has given me the greatest satisfaction I've ever had from driving. I love getting behind the wheel and using all the gadgets in it. I've had other cars in the past that, just to remember driving them, makes me moan because the experience was so miserable. While you're doing an internship, ask yourself the question: Do I look forward to getting up and getting into this car (or internship)? On the weekends, I do volunteer work in which I use my car and I'm delighted to do so because I love driving it. Similarly, when people ask me to come and give a lecture to an organization that's doing great work, I gladly do it without compensation. It's like driving a car you love getting into. Your gift does not have to be the basis of a paid profession. It can be, but you love doing it so much you would do it for free. I look at internships in part as a way of identifying, vetting, and examining what you think your gift is. You won't have to guess anymore. It'll be as obvious as a gigantic grizzly bear in the middle of a country road in the daytime. There will be no way of not seeing it.

My undergraduate degree is in physical education. When I was earning that degree, I wanted to use my gift to serve others as a teacher and coach. During summer vacations, I worked at lacrosse camps that exposed me to the profession and gave me the opportunity to network with great coaches—many of them teachers, too. I got exposure to teachers and coaches at different levels so I could learn which would be the appropriate age group for me to use my gift with. Someone's gift as an elementary schoolteacher would be an absolute flop at the high school level. Before graduating, my degree program required participating in teacher observations, which allowed me to spend time in the classroom with experienced teachers who shared with me all aspects of their job.

In the last year my degree program required that I do student teaching. This gave me time shadowing experienced teachers and then the opportunity to teach a class solo. At first it was terrifying, but it gave me the necessary repetitions (reps) to work on my teaching skills. Reps are the practice of a set of skills necessary to gain mastery and expertise at something whether it be teaching, public speaking, editing, writing, creating, or diagnosing a problem. Malcolm Gladwell talks about this in his book *Outliers,* in which he looks at the theory that to develop competence in a particular field or skill you must have about 10,000 hours of practice.[38] That's what internships do: they help you gain the necessary reps to perfect your gifts. Whether you're studying to be a realtor, contractor, locksmith, entrepreneur, or professor, you need exposure to what the experts do. The more you work with the best, the better prepared you're going to be when the curtain goes up, such as during an interview or pitch to receive an income-producing opportunity to serve others with your gift. What's a pitch? Quickly and tactfully introducing yourself, sharing how your gift can solve a problem, stating a positive outcome your gift can generate, providing proof and a plan, and listening to the catcher's feedback.

As a college professor, I regularly serve as a reference for students applying for internships, so I know a bit about the process and the experience. I have learned that the students who have had internships before their senior year are more often than not the ones who, before the end of their last semester in college, have a job signed, sealed, and delivered. Why? Because today internships are the process that employers use to screen potential hires. The internship works like a farm team in professional sports. It gives the company the ability to evaluate the character of a person over a long period of time. They're looking at questions such as: Does this person give their best effort? Does this person do the right thing because it's the right thing to do? Is this person a good teammate or colleague? You can fake that for a week but not over six weeks. The truth will come out, be it bad or good. Second, the internship gives you the ability to check out an industry and/or company. You can save yourself a lot of time and retraining by doing an internship.

As a senior in college, I seriously considered becoming a podiatrist. During my first year in high school, I had a painful foot injury that made me aware that I needed orthotics to address being flat-footed and having bunions. If you've ever had bunions you know that they will give you an excruciating pain when they get bumped with a hard object or surface even slightly. After my freshman year in college, the podiatrist that I had been seeing performed surgery on me to remove the increasingly painful bunions. This experience, along with observing the luxurious lifestyle of my podiatrist, piqued my interest in the profession. I contacted my podiatrist and did what I have come to call a career interview, which allows you to learn more about someone's requirements and training to practice in their field. My doctor suggested that I come and shadow him as an introduction to what it meant to be a podiatrist.

This is where the story gets interesting and why I stress the importance of internships, paid or unpaid, as well as opportunities to shadow a person with experience in the field you are considering for a career. The day I shadowed my podiatrist he had a minor surgery scheduled in his office. I observed his bedside manner, his preparation for surgery, and his injection of a local anesthetic to numb the area he would be working on. Then he took a scalpel out of a sanitized package and began an incision that naturally led to bleeding. The next thing I knew I was coming to outside his office after fainting at the sight of the blood. I am not joking! That was a very inexpensive and time-saving method for me to learn that I was not cut out (I couldn't resist the pun) for the field of podiatry. If you're gifted in the necessities of a particular career, an internship will confirm that.

I've had a handful of friends who played lacrosse at Cornell University. They tell me that players on the lacrosse team enjoy the benefit of summer internships on Wall Street in New York City working at some of the top firms, such as Goldman Sachs. Those internships led to careers on Wall Street after they completed their four years of playing eligibility and they obtained their college degrees. If you know anything about investment banking, you will find that it is filled with former collegiate lacrosse players from some of the top programs in the country. Can you imagine the networking that goes on during those summer internships? Interns are exposed to the various jobs and opportunities that exist at a firm, interact with employees at all different levels, and take in the work that people perform, the relationships they have, and the compensation they receive. I knew of a student athlete at Wellesley College who, the summer before her senior year, worked at one of the top investment banks on Wall Street. She and the other college interns with whom she worked were either offered a job at the firm or not by the start of their senior year. Think about the peace you would feel going into your senior year in college knowing you had secured your first job, where you would be living, and what your starting salary and benefits would be.

The same is true of a person who interns as a pharmacist for Walgreens, CVS, or Rite Aid. It's also true for the person enrolled in a program to become a locksmith and working for a locksmith part-time on the side. If you're working with a good one you will learn how to run a small business successfully and how to troubleshoot all manner of problems as you travel with that locksmith on calls. In more than one of Anthony Bourdain's books on his career as a professional chef, he advises anyone thinking about going into the culinary arts to work in a professional kitchen for six months. If you like that experience, he suggests, then and only then should you enroll in a culinary school. You also learn that after graduating from culinary school the best chefs pursue what they call stages—the culinary version of what a medical student calls a residency. Often, the chef will do two or three stages with some of the best in their field. If they're good, the chef they work under will use their contacts to open better career opportunities for the chef in training.

I asked a student in medical school what she would suggest to those interested in a career as a doctor or surgeon. This is what she said:

> Many of the classmates in my program come from families of medical doctors. They came into medical school familiar with the jargon related to the profession and an understanding of the ABCs of becoming a healthcare practitioner. I didn't have that advantage and I've had to play catch-up. I would suggest that a person volunteer in hospitals and take any other steps they can find to become familiar with the profession.

That suggestion is a good transition to talk about volunteer opportunities related to how you want to use your gift to serve others. Anytime you get a chance to be exposed to a related career, take advantage of it. Experience is as valuable as a paycheck in many instances. The following story is a case in point.

I interviewed Ohio State Head Lacrosse Coach Nick Myers for my podcast, *The Fred Opie Show*. I asked him to share his decision and journey to becoming the head lacrosse coach of a Big Ten school. First, he pointed to the fact that he grew up with his stepfather, a dedicated high school coach and teacher whose example inspired him in part to go into coaching. Myers attended Springfield College, which has produced outstanding teachers and coaches for decades including Mike Woicik. The key for him had been working at lacrosse camps during summer vacations while he attended college. But here's the clincher. He served as an assistant college coach and in paid positions for several years. But volunteering on the Ohio State lacrosse coaching staff is what he attributes to ultimately landing him a paid position as a first assistant and then giving him the opportunity to interview for and obtain the head coach position years later. Did you hear that, folks? A volunteer job! Translation: the guy worked for free!

I liken internships and volunteer opportunities to aircraft simulators. Let me explain what I mean. My friend and high school teammate, Joe Vasta, played lacrosse at the Air Force Academy. After an outstanding playing career, he served as a fighter pilot in the US Air Force. Today he's a civilian pilot working for FedEx. Throughout his career as a pilot, he has had to learn to fly new aircraft. These cost hundreds of thousands, if not millions, of dollars. Before the US government and FedEx allowed Joe to fly one of these expensive babies, they trained him how to do so safely on what they call a flight simulator, a machine built to look just like the cockpit of a real plane. It has a screen that shows what looks like a real runway and then the sky when you're up in the air. Joe tells me that the simulator is set up to ready you for all kinds of real-life situation circumstances and emergencies. The trainers put you through numerous scenarios to prepare you for the real thing, and you don't graduate to the real thing until you can do it in the simulator. They tell me that pilots can go through training in a simulator that is so rigorous and stressful that when they come out they're sweaty, have the jitters, and feel like they crashed the plane for real.

But that's what an internship or volunteer experience can do for you. It allows you to go through all kinds of situations that will prepare you for using your gift to serve others and make a profitable income and, Lord willing, keep you from crashing your career down the road. If done correctly the internship and volunteer experience will say to potential employers that this person is ready to fly successfully with their company or institution. When should you look for a volunteer opportunity or internship? Take a cue from the medical student: as early as possible. It will give you on-the-job experience to know if this is the right vehicle for you to use your gift to serve others and make an income.

Like I said, internships give you the ability to test-drive your career before you commit to a college major or a job. They help you learn new skills and build a network of colleagues as well as take a chance on something new.[39]

Use the Internet to learn more about the organization or company that you're considering interning with. Also, interview people who work at the place where you want to intern. A good question to ask is, "What are the challenges facing this organization or industry today and in the future?"

## Getting the Most from an Internship

Here are three suggestions on how to get the most out of your internship:

1. Carve out a project that will help you get the most out of your internship.
2. Learn what the critical skills are and the language used in your field.[40]
3. Keep your eyes and ears open, get a mentor, and learn everything you can from others where you're interning. Take as many notes as possible; consider journaling about your internship as a way of documenting your experience.

Look for opportunities to leverage your gift and abilities to serve the place where you are interning and the supervisor you report to. A great intern looks for opportunities to solve problems. Whatever you do, do it in such a way that you make those who you represent look good (1 Corinthians 10:31). Another one of my mantras is do the right thing because it's the right thing to do. And do the right thing even when people aren't looking; if you do so you are sure to get ahead in life and your career.

It's critical to remember that internships provide great ways for you to build the skills needed for your future success.[41] For example, I'm working hard to increase the size of my podcast audience. In the process, I have to learn how to cross-pollinate my podcast with others, collaborate with other podcasters in my area of expertise, understand why a particular podcast attracts large numbers of listeners, and learn how to use social media to distribute my podcast. This a skill set that I have to learn and exercise.

## Speaking and Writing

The most common fear that people have is public speaking. To be in front of people delivering a message can simply unnerve some, if not most, folks. It makes you feel completely naked because you can't hide when everybody's looking at you. Similarly, some folks suffer from writer's block—the inability to get your message across on paper. Being able to speak and write well are critical to obtaining a great internship opportunity.[42]

As I write this, it's that time of the semester when my students are doing presentations in which they share the findings of their research. As I listen to them deliver their content, I mark those who need to improve their public speaking ability, and I recommend that they join the organization Toastmasters, a self-help association where one can learn how to improve their public speaking skills.

My wife is also a college professor. She has a technique she uses to get people out of the habit of saying "um" when they speak. She has an empty coffee can when they're practicing their public speaking into which she drops a coin every time the student fills empty space in their talk with "um." It's unsettling and a good motivator for improving their speaking skills.

Another important part of public speaking is varying your cadence; you must avoid a monotone level of talking that makes you sound like a computer. Be enthusiastic, and raise and lower your voice to make your point and keep your audience engaged. I've mentioned this before but it bears repeating: if you have trouble with public speaking, get your reps. To get your reps, consider joining an organization like Toastmasters.

I do a lot of interviews as the host of a podcast. It's very impressive when I interview someone who can clearly express their point of view because not everyone can. To me, there's nothing better than someone who is simply profound. It's not about using fancy words. Listening to a poor communicator is like listening to a radio station that won't come in clearly because of excessive static and interference. It makes it very hard to understand the person speaking.

Similarly, you want to continue to work on your writing skills, because the people who write and speak well will get more opportunities. To improve your writing, I suggest you start a blog on something you're passionate about. Set a goal of writing one great paragraph per day and you will inevitably improve your writing. Practice writing using active verbs. If that makes no sense to you, then I suggest you get a copy of Stephen King's book *On Writing*.[43]

**Team/Group Work**

The ability to work well in teams is critical to your success as an intern and in life. I started assigning group projects in the courses I teach about three years ago for many reasons, but one of them is that I understood what an important skill it is for my students to get along with others. A peer-evaluation component represents a percentage of the student's final grade. And guess what, many jobs have annual evaluations that include peer reviews. All my students take peer review surveys, and they are asked three types of questions:

1. Is this person a pleasure to work with?
2. Does he/she make important contributions to deliverables?
3. Does he/she show up on time and prepared to work?

A person with great teamwork skills will quickly be noticed in an internship, and that will lead them to job opportunities as well as affirmative responses to requests for recommendations. I also tell my students that you never know when you're going to meet a person again with whom you worked on a team during your undergraduate experience. How do you want that future encounter to go? You can determine your future outcome through your current behavior and effort.[44]

**Enthusiasm**

Enthusiasm is a sign that you are truly interested in the internship that you are participating in. As a professor, when I look around a classroom and see one of my students looking as if Eeyore in Winnie-the-Pooh stories is their spirit animal, I know there's a problem. But the student who is fired up and excited about being in class is positively influencing their final grade. The same is true on the practice field. If you look like a sad sack when you come to practice, do you think you have a good chance to get into the game in a critical situation, if at all? If you're not enthusiastic about what you are doing, you need to ask yourself if this is the right internship for you. I'm not saying every day's going to feel like the Oscars, but neither should it feel like preseason football practice in Junction, Texas, under football coach Paul "Bear" Bryant. A former member of his squad, Jim Dent, tells the story about how, as the new Texas A&M head football coach in 1954, Bryan made his players undergo twice-a-day practices in one-hundred-plus-degree heat in August and Spartan conditions.[45] Equally, you want to stretch your comfort zone to learn everything you need about a particular industry. I like the saying, "You can be committed or comfortable." A great intern seeks out all those areas where they have weaknesses and tries to work on them and get better at the essential skills needed to use their gift and make a great income in the process. That's what I've had to do to continue to develop and maintain my Spanish language skills. It means that if I want to develop my skills I talk to native speakers on a regular basis and am willing to make mistakes and look stupid in the process.

It's the same thing in basketball and lacrosse. If you want to be great you need to work hard at becoming ambidextrous; it's the only way you're going to get better. I was an assistant lacrosse coach at Gettysburg College for several years. My players would watch me shoot on our goaltenders to warm them up for practices and games. They would ask me, "Coach, are you right-handed or left-handed?" To challenge them, I would say, "You tell me." I tried to put it in their head that if they worked hard enough on their non-dominant hand they could get to the point where people couldn't tell whether they were right-handed or left-handed when they shot or passed.

You want the same thing to happen with your essential skills in your industry. You want to be so good that people can't tell the areas that you spent so much time working on that they seem almost flawless. I just complimented one of my students at the end of the semester on her work effort. I told her that she was diligent, which I defined as someone who consistently moves toward excellence. It doesn't mean you're perfect. It means you are striving to get better and better every day, pushing yourself with maximum effort. Those are the people who get ahead in their careers. Don't just go through the motions as an intern. Be diligent![46]

**Impressions**

I was first hired as an assistant history professor at Morehouse College in Atlanta, Georgia. Nobel Prize winner Martin Luther King Jr., Atlanta Mayor Maynard Jackson, US Surgeon General David Satcher, Olympian Edwin Moses, Academy Award-winning actor Samuel L. Jackson, and filmmaker Spike Lee are just a few of the many noted Morehouse alumni. Morehouse had a mantra we conveyed to our students: To be early is to be on time, to be on time is to be late, and to be late is an abomination. Remember that and it will take you a long way in your career. If first impressions when you walk into a new internship are good, lasting impressions when the internship is over are even more important. If during a four-week internship you show up on time, do what you say you're going to do, and submit your deliverables on time, you're going to make a lasting impression and get ahead in one way or another. Why? Because most folks simply don't have the discipline necessary to keep their word. Normal people are most often like granola— they are flaky, nutty, and fruity. I've also observed that most people suffer from low self-esteem, which results in: (1) folks running roughshod over them because they don't establish healthy boundaries, and (2) folks who are insecure, which manifests itself in cocky behavior. Instead, I encourage you to do the inside-out work to establish a quiet confidence and become who God has created you to be in the gifts he has given you.[47] If you're having problems establishing healthy boundaries with people a great book is Dr. Henry Cloud's *Boundaries: When to Say Yes, How to Say No to Take Control of Your Life*.

What are some things you can do going into your internship to bolster your self-confidence and make an excellent impression in the process? Here are three strategies I use, which spell the word "red":

**R**ead: inspiring stories about those who have overcome and how to get better

**E**xercise and **E**at well: release endorphins and eat to win

**D**ress and groom for success: be prepared for opportunities

Comedian Steve Harvey has written a book titled *Act Like a Success, Think Like a Success: Discovering Your Gift and the Way to Life's Riches*. Read, exercise, eat, dress, and groom like a success and your self-confidence will increase and stay at a high level. You want to be an outstanding intern—someone who stands out among the other interns. How do you do that? Be self-confident and be a person of integrity, give your best effort, and show that you care. It's just that simple. And if you want to be even more outstanding, then come to the internship table with "SMART" goals.

## Goals

You want to come to the internship with goals because, without them, you are like the person who fills up their gas tank, gets the car tuned up, gets it washed, and then jumps on the highway and starts driving without a GPS destination. Internship goals allow you to determine what you want to get out of the experience and exposure. To do that, I want you to create SMART goals, which are defined as:

**S**avvy: specific and easy-to-understand

**M**easurable: clearly defined to demonstrate what you want to achieve

**A**ctive: action-oriented with verbs such as meet, present, and create

**R**eachable: realistic and obtainable

**T**imed: grounded by a set timeline

I created a SMART goal to complete this book. I wanted to create a book of about two hundred pages or less in length. In terms of action, I set a goal of working on it for one hour each Tuesday, Thursday, and Friday, which were nonteaching days for me during the academic year, and every day when not teaching, such as during winter breaks and summer vacation. I had written several books before, so I knew that this was a realistic and attainable goal. And I planned to have the book completed and published by the end of 2017. You can establish and complete SMART goals. And once you achieve one, the others will come even more easily because now you have experience.

# CHAPTER 5

# Get a Job

## Vehicles and Outlets

It's never too late to discover and accept the gift that God has given you. And it's never too late to change what you're doing and put yourself in a position to use your gift to serve others and make a better income in the process. After you discover and develop your gift, look around for the best vehicles and outlets for your gift. Those outlets are everywhere around you, so get started where you are. In this chapter, I use Steve Harvey's paradigm in his book *Act Like a Success*, in which he discusses jobs as vehicles that take you from one place to the other to best use your gift to serve others and make a living.

Your first vehicle will most likely not be the one you're driving when your journey comes to an end. Attach yourself to a vehicle that gets your journey in motion from where you are to where you want to go. The mentors in your life can help you understand where your gift can and cannot take you. Remember to always transfer up in your choice of vehicle. You want to move closer to first class with each transfer, meaning that your compensation should increase and your opportunities should get better.

I first starting teaching and addressing audiences at camps and in churches. I used to accept invitations that paid $100. Now I receive a whole lot more than that. That doesn't stop me from using my gift for free if I choose to do so. And I've had to learn how to say no to lower compensation so as to keep my calendar open to higher-paying opportunities. The natural progression for my gift has been—and should be—camps, classrooms, lecture halls, radio, television, documentaries, keynote speeches.

What about you? Try mapping out the natural progression of your gift with a mentor. Be open to a vehicle that complements the current level of your gift but can promote you to the next level appropriate to it. Start now where you are. What can you do today to begin the journey using your gift where you are? What first steps and/or vehicle can you identify and get moving? For me, I worked at lacrosse camps, where I got the opportunity to teach young campers as well as the entire camp, including players and coaches. Are you open to feedback and willing to get a mentor who can guide you? Learning from those driving a better vehicle is always a great idea.

Keep working hard in the vehicle you are in now to catch another transfer. Keep looking for a better transfer and take them as often as possible, avoiding foolish risk-taking in the process. As the old saying goes, the best way to eat an elephant is one bite at a time; and you run a marathon only one step at a time. Start with local vehicles first, then expand outside your area. Let your vehicle teach you how to drive and patiently learn everything you can about it before moving up to a better vehicle. Master it and make every mistake you can in an old jalopy before you get into a shiny Porsche Cayenne GTS.

## The Right Space for Your Gift

You may have the gift of service, but you don't have to resign yourself to working in nonprofit organizations doing charity work. The service sector of our economy is large and lucrative. For those with the gift of service, you can make out like a bandit without going to jail. I always tell people that I like my job so much that I should put a mask on when I go to cash my check at the bank because I feel like I'm stealing (except when I'm grading papers!). If you have the gift of service, you might consider getting into the hotel, resort, or country club business, and a whole host of other places where people go to relax and be served. I don't know if you have noticed, but you pay good money to relax in those spaces, so somebody's getting paid.

If you are like me and have the gift of teaching, you should figure out whether you should be teaching at a public or private school. What level of student should you be teaching? Should you teach on the radio or TV?

Could you teach in a correctional facility? Should you teach as a tour guide? There are many places where you can teach. Perhaps you should teach as a corporate trainer showing employees how to do their job. It all depends on what will give you the most satisfaction, and nobody can answer that question but you.

I am a professor of history, the author of books and articles, a public speaker, and a contributor on radio and television. These are all outlets for me to teach, which is what I have been gifted to do. It all started with my first job in Danbury, Connecticut. I love the way Steve Harvey views the jobs he has had over the course of his career once he learned that he had the gift and talent to be a comedian. Harvey views jobs as vehicles to help get your gift from one space and venue to another. A job is a stepping-stone to get you to the best and most appropriate spaces for you to use your gift to serve others and make an income. Let's talk about my first one in Danbury, Connecticut.

After completing my undergraduate physical education requirements, I accepted a job teaching and coaching in Danbury, where I taught kindergarten through seventh grade for two years and coached boys' junior varsity soccer and middle school boys' basketball. The teaching and coaching experiences were tremendous, and I learned how to get my lessons across to young children in the classroom and to middle and high school students as a coach.

But Danbury didn't have a lacrosse program then, and my goal had been to obtain a position where I would teach and coach a varsity lacrosse team. A teaching and coaching position opened up in Hempstead, New York, on Long Island, so I took it. I started teaching physical education and coaching at the high school. This gave me valuable experience teaching in a predominantly African American school district that, at the time, had a lot of challenges: some students coming from unstable homes, a school district operating on an austerity budget, and the temptation for adolescents to make fast money selling drugs. Hempstead was a rough place to be a teacher, but I gained valuable experience in how to teach in different environments and how to gain people's confidence and trust.

I made a lot of mistakes as a teacher and coach during my year at Hempstead High School, but I learned from those mistakes and they've helped me become the teacher and parent I am today.

After the high school teaching and coaching job, I next went to work at Gettysburg College and graduate school at Shippensburg University to obtain a master's degree in history. While in graduate school, I gained additional teaching experience teaching a course at Gettysburg College. I also had a job as interim dean. The interim dean position provided a great opportunity for me to learn whether higher education administration would be a good fit for my gift, talents, and abilities.

I've been an educator for more than thirty years and a college professor for almost twenty of those years. During that time, I have passed up numerous opportunities to apply for administration jobs. I passed them up because I remembered the time I worked as an interim dean; I learned then that administration wasn't for me. More recently I've come to reconsider being a school administrator as a possible vehicle for me in which I could mentor less experienced teachers. It's important to know the kind of work that gives you fulfillment day in and day out. Understanding that about myself has helped me evaluate vehicle options for my gift.

After that year as an interim dean at Gettysburg College, I completed my graduate school studies at Syracuse University. While in graduate school, I had numerous jobs. I worked as a graduate assistant with several different professors who had small discussion groups. I graded papers and held office hours with students. Those jobs were invaluable and gave me hands-on experience as a college professor. I also worked about ten hours a week selling athletic footwear at Dick's Sporting Goods. That job provided an opportunity for me to develop sales skills, customer service skills, and gain exposure to life in corporate America. I call upon the skills I learned while selling athletic footwear when I am promoting a new book and interacting with people interested in learning more about it and those who end up buying the book and asking me to sign it. The customer service skills I learned back at Dick's Sporting Goods have been invaluable to me as an author.

Another interesting job I had along my journey after graduate school was teaching Spanish at a private high school in the Washington, DC, area. As I previously mentioned, I learned Spanish as part of my graduate school requirements. As a graduate student, I spent summers studying Spanish in Mexico. I also did several months of fieldwork in Guatemala City to research and write my PhD dissertation. I took a job teaching Spanish to maintain my language skills and to pay bills while I spent the year writing the dissertation. The teaching job was great for preparing me to be a college professor. As a Spanish teacher, I had to create daily lesson plans, homework assignments, quizzes, and exams for my students and manage lots of grading. These are skills I use today as a college professor.

After completing my graduate degree, I took my first job as a college professor at Morehouse College in Atlanta, where I had to learn how to negotiate, and I made a lot of mistakes that I have not since repeated. My time at Morehouse helped me develop critical skills as a college professor, including classroom management; syllabus, quiz, and exam creation; how to give students clear feedback on assignments and exams; how to teach research and writing; and selecting and ordering reading content for a course. I also learned how to manage the requirements necessary for gaining tenure as a professor. One must be able to manage the demands of teaching a course, publishing original content, and serving on committees. What I learned at Morehouse has helped me through the tenure process and to coach junior colleagues as well.

The best piece of advice I can give to anybody choosing between numerous job options is to lean toward the job opportunity that will give you more opportunities thereafter, even if it means you might receive a little bit less compensation for that job. For example, I left Morehouse to take a job at Marist College because of the opportunity it provided me and my family. The new job increased my salary and gave me the chance to be the director of a new program: I was hired with the charge of creating an area studies program. That came to fruition and Marist now has a minor that never existed before in African Diaspora Studies. As part of that process, I designed and taught a new related course. I incorporated the library's digital content and created a fully integrated hot-linked syllabus that allowed students to open all the required course readings digitally.

While at Marist, I also participated in the college's Teaching American History Institutes, in which I created several graduate history courses. I also gained more time and support for research and writing. In the meantime, my wife had decided she wanted to explore the possibility of teaching at the college level. I negotiated a new position for her as a Marist College Presidential Fellow. She spent a year at the college, during which she taught a course in the business school and shadowed college president Dennis Murray. This gave my wife the opportunity to experience what it would be like to be a college professor and/or administrator.

I also was able to negotiate an opportunity to teach a course in Cuba as part of the college's study abroad program. The opportunity to go to Cuba was important because one of my areas of specialization is Latin America, of which Cuba is a part. During that research trip to Cuba, I taught a course for Marist students and used some of my free time to do extensive archival research in Havana. An additional reason why the new job had been a good fit is that it allowed me to return to the Hudson Valley where I grew up. At the time, our first child was barely two years old and the relocation would allow him to get to know his grandparents and other family members on my side of the family.

I spent seven years at Marist College, during which I established a new minor and a program on campus and created and taught new classes. My reduced teaching load and the increased support for research and writing allowed me to publish sufficiently to gain tenure and put me in position to go on to publish my next two books and several other articles. Much of the groundwork I needed to get promoted to full professor occurred during the years I spent at Marist. My wife's time at Marist helped her decide to pursue a career as a college professor. She applied to New York University (NYU) and gained admission and support to complete a PhD. Also, during the last years of our time at Marist and New York University, my father was diagnosed with leukemia. We were able to support him and my mother as he went through treatment and spend quality time with him as a family during his last days.

During the last year at Marist and NYU, my wife received a job offer from Babson College and I received a job offer from University of Tennessee at Knoxville. How did we make the decision to accept the offer at Babson? I used my network to learn what the best job opportunity for us both would be. Babson College had a superior business school, and during the negotiation process, school administrators brought me on campus for an interview as a faculty hire—something that's not easy to accomplish but not unusual in higher ed. By this time, I had become a tenured associate professor with a strong teaching and publishing record. We also had our second child while living in New York. Negotiations went well and we decided to come to Massachusetts, where we have both teach. In each instance, I had the leverage, the knowledge, and the support of mentors to decide which job would provide the most opportunities in the long run.

A job truly is like a vehicle: it takes you from one place to another. As your income improves, so should the car you drive. Similarly, as you develop your gift, you should have improved opportunities to use it and be better compensated for it. If you're in a significant relationship like a marriage, you must make decisions that are best for the entire family. Since getting hitched, I have consistently chosen jobs that have been in the best interest of my wife and family. Each time I have done this it has caused my career opportunities to improve and our household income to increase. I also left Atlanta for New York because I knew that the public schools in New York were better than those in the area of Atlanta where we lived. Similarly, the decision to come to Massachusetts was in part because we knew we could put our kids in excellent schools.

When looking at a job you must factor in the benefits package the employer is offering, the cost of living, and how the new job and location would meet your lifestyle demands. My first teaching job in Danbury, Connecticut, meant an almost one-hour commute from home to work. That commute has stuck with me and I have done everything in my power thereafter to have a short commute to work if it meant I had to drive. In Atlanta, we purchased a home within a thirty-minute bike ride or a fifteen-minute commute on public transportation to my job. When we moved to New York we bought a home that was a five-minute walk from the commuter train station. The location allowed my wife to get to NYU within forty-five minutes. I purchased a fold-up bike that I took on the train heading north for approximately one hour and then a ten-minute bike ride to work from the train station. I made the sacrifice so my wife would have a shorter commute to school. I made the best of it and I learned to enjoy the commute on the train, which ran along the banks of the Hudson River. That train ride to work allowed me to take in picturesque sunrises and sunsets and to spend some productive time researching and writing books and articles, grading papers, eating meals, and catching up on sleep. When we moved to Massachusetts we rented a home for the first several years to be sure this was the right fit for us in terms of employment and living arrangements. I had a fifteen-minute bike ride to work!

**Idella Hansen and Sandi Talbott:** Idella Hansen (age sixty-six) started driving big rig trucks in 1968 at the age of eighteen. In search of independence, she got behind the wheel of her first truck and never looked back. After driving for more than forty years, she and her best friend, Sandi Talbott (age seventy-five), also a long-time truck driver, reflected on their vocation:

Hansen: Can you imagine doing anything else, Sandi?
Talbott: Absolutely not. Four years ago, I had a heart attack while I was on the truck. And when I got ready to go back on the road, I pulled out of my driveway and started through the gear pattern, it was like I'm back in my element. It is my life.
Hansen: I'm not interested in getting out of it. I'm not interested in retiring. When I get in that seat, instead of being slump-shouldered, all of a sudden, I have sat up straight, pulled my shoulders back, and it's like a rush of hot blood.

Talbott: I'm like you, Idella. Don't talk to me about cooking meals. I certainly don't wanna clean. But what if something happens to my health? What am I going to do?
Hansen: I'll stuff you in the truck with me.
Talbott: [laughs] When they pry our cold dead fingers off the wheel that's when we'll retire... because when people retire, they die. And we ain't ready for that.
Hansen: Hopefully, I'll be one of them you find sitting behind the wheel somewhere. I'm not interested in going home. I just want to drive my truck.
Talbott: Right.
Hansen: That's what I want to do. I want to drive my truck.

My message is: A job is a lot more than salary; it's a lifestyle. You want to be sure that you're happy with as many aspects of your job as possible and the geography associated with it. Are you going somewhere with places of worship, shopping, and friends in which you can recreate a sense of community? Do the recreational outlets and opportunities meet your needs? These are all things one must consider in addition to what a job offers that allow you to serve others with your gift and earn a good income.

I love companies dedicated to the personal development of its employees. Companies where employees are able to attend conferences and professional opportunities in their field. Having that kind of support makes us better at what we do. We also grow professionally when we work with the best and brightest colleagues; it's the biblical principal that *iron sharpens iron* (read Proverbs 27:17). Great colleagues in a great work environment push us to be better at what we do. As an athlete, I got better at my sport as I played with and around better players. Similarly, you will become better as a professional in your career as you surround yourself with better experts in your field.

In terms of jobs, you want to be in a position in which you are not the smartest person in your department. If you are reluctant to be learning from others around you, you want to be able to allow a colleague's iron to sharpen your iron. I would rather be around samurai swords than butter knives. A fellowship at Harvard University served as one of the greatest opportunities I have had professionally. It gave me an entire academic year to do a deep dive on a book project. The fellowship came with office space, research assistants, and library privileges at Harvard. For me, access to Harvard's research libraries is equivalent to giving a fifth grader free reign in Willy

Wonka's chocolate factory!

Additionally, I spent that year with ten or so other fellows working on their own research. These folks can best be described as scholars at the top of their field, and they supported and encouraged my work and I theirs. At the end of that year, I was a better writer and researcher and a much better speaker. Once a week we attended a research talk in which one of us presented our work and then entertained questions about our findings and/or our craft. Other days we had the opportunity to listen to others, like Toni Morrison, who came in to share their work. Seek opportunities like these that will allow and encourage you to grow and better use your gift to serve others and make a great income.

## Upgrading

Don't get stuck in the current vehicle that you're driving for too long. If you are working very hard in your current vehicle and you start to see a lack of opportunity or progress in developing your skills, it's time for an upgrade. It's time to take another class, join a new organization, find another vehicle, or start a new business. If you're perfecting your vehicle and working hard to get better, then you'll know when it's time for a new one. It's a lot like church growth. Elders should not vote on constructing a new building until they're busting out of the one they're currently in. Ask yourself if you have maxed out every opportunity for growth and development in your vehicle. Is the trunk jam-packed full? Do you have stuff on the floors, attached to the roof, in all the storage spaces? If so, it's time for an upgrade to a larger vehicle. In my case, I had to know when it was time to leave the different institutions where I had worked. I had to know when it's time to stop accepting speaking invites under a certain amount, when to stop publishing with academic presses, and when to stop accepting interview requests from certain media outlets.

**Harnarayan Singh:** *Hockey Night in Canada* broadcaster Harnarayan Singh applied to and graduated from a broadcasting school. From there, he went on to take a job as a local news reporter for a radio station where he worked for several years and during that time consistently pitched hockey stories to his editors. His first break came when Joel Darling, the executive producer of the show, called him. He told Singh that he had learned about his passion for broadcasting ice hockey and his Punjabi language skills. He was the right candidate for the show's interest in launching a broadcast in Punjabi. It turned out that after English and French, Punjabi served as Canada's third most highly spoken language. For several years, Singh called games in Punjabi below the radar of most of the hockey world. And he made great sacrifices to turn the opportunity from a part-time gig to making enough for him to quit his day job and end a weekly, 1,600-mile commute that he paid for himself and which took a toll on his health (*that part I am not endorsing*). Over time, his show grew in popularity and it moved closer to where he lived, ending his exhausting weekly commute. After nearly ten years of broadcasting NHL games in Punjabi, Singh caught a break during last year's Stanley Cup finals when he called the goal that went viral on social media. *Singh became a more-than-fifteen-year overnight success.* This season he has gained additional well-compensated opportunities to use his gift to serve others in addition to his regular NHL broadcast in Punjabi, including doing ringside reporting for other national broadcasters of NHL games.[48]

## Test-Drive

Choose vehicles that will get you to higher levels. Let's move beyond thinking about traditional nine-to-five jobs. Take the time to test-drive as many options as you can for your gift. In my case, at the time of writing this book, I started testing out doing webinars as a way of promoting the books I've written and the trainings that I've put together over the years but have only shared with the students in my courses. It required me to take the steps to learn how to use webinar software and equipment and everything else related to making it work. I have to come up with incentives for people to sign up for the webinars and then to buy a book or training that I offer. For example, there are several thrift shops that I frequent that give customers a frequent shopper card, stamping the card for each visit in which customers spend five dollars or more. Once the card is filled with ten stamps, the customer gets a percentage off their next purchase to be used toward two specific store items only. This repeat customer incentive has me going back with my frequent shopper card in my wallet.

Your vehicle can be as unique as your gift, and it may allow you to have several jobs at the same time. For example, I'm a college professor, public speaker, conference organizer, contributor to shows, author, coach, and podcast host. In my case, I need to remember to discipline myself to drive in vehicles that accentuate my research and teaching skills, intellectual curiosity, and curating, analytical, writing, and verbal skills. Don't be afraid to test-drive a car outside your price range. Don't let the time, training, distance, or other requirements keep you from considering an upgrade.

## Don't Get Stuck

You need to recognize the type of vehicles that are suitable for your gifts and the ones that are not. Think hard about the vehicle you're considering getting into before you do it. Should you be coaching high school, college, or pro sports? Should you rent space in someone else's restaurant, get a food truck, open a stand, or work in somebody else's restaurant? Do you have the right team around you for the vehicle you're considering driving for this season? Take the time to network with people in your field and find out the time, money, and other sacrifices it takes to successfully drive the vehicles that you're considering. Ask those who are ahead of you in the field you're interested in about the types of vehicles they drove before they got into their current one. Ask them about the type of time and money necessary to drive this one. How often are they away from home, and what kind of stress does it put on their life? Ask about the other type of stressors that comes with driving this vehicle.

> **Sharon Long:** In the 1970s, single mom Sharon Long worked several jobs Monday through Sunday to provide for her two kids. She found the work dissatisfying and exhausting but she did it to pay the bills. At the age of forty, she was helping her oldest daughter register for college. In the process, Long met a college financial aid officer who she told just how much she hated the work that she had been doing to meet her family's needs. The financial aid officer convinced Long to enroll in a degree program in which she could change her career. Not only did she convince Long but she helped her complete the necessary paperwork. And at age forty, Long enrolled in an art degree program. The program had a science requirement that led Long to take a physical anthropology course. It was in that class that Long identified and began to develop her gift as a forensic artist (recreating human faces from skulls). After

earning a degree, she went on to use her gift in a number of spaces such as museums, law enforcement agencies, National Geographic Society, Smithsonian, The History Channel, and *America's Most Wanted* television program.

At age seventy-five, Sharon Long explained the experience of discovering her gift and monetizing it over her career. She says, "When I took that anthropology class, I learned at age forty what I want to be when I grow up." She goes on to explain the energy level and the natural high that one gets as the right kind of endorphins flow when you're using your gifts and ability to serve others. It's why I say it feels like your vocation is a vacation. "I get totally psyched into what I'm doing. Just like people must do when they're writing music or painting a painting. You forget to eat, you forget to get up, you forget to drink water, you forget everything. Everything just sort of goes into suspension," when I'm in the zone and the creative juices within me flow "out of the tips of my fingers" as I'm working.[49]

## Cars and Careers

Here are three questions that will help you choose the right vehicle for your gift:

1. Where is your final destination? Always keep your long-term goals in mind and make strategic decisions that lead you in that direction. Focus on positioning yourself to acquire the skills and relationships that will bear fruit in the years to come. Those who fall for get-rich-quick schemes get fleeced or shortchanged in the long run. Good mentors in your life can help you make strategic long-term decisions that will get you closer to your desired final destination.

2. Where is your next stop? Look at your career as having phases and stages. There are stages in which you can invest a great amount of time into building your career. There are stages in which you need to put more time into more important priorities. Maybe some of the things that you want to do career-wise need to wait for now. Perhaps it needs to wait until you have more discretionary dollars to invest in your career. It's similar to being an athlete. Your fitness and conditioning training is different during the preseason, in

season, and out of season. You can't train in the same way during these different seasons. Your body needs time to rest and relax, and there are times your body needs to be stressed and/or strengthened and times when you need to maintain but not increase your fitness level while you're in season. Likewise, how you use your gift has similar seasons.

3. Do you know how to operate this vehicle just enough not to crash it? The right vehicle better utilizes your gift and increases your earnings. It should be challenging, fun, and take you out of your comfort zone. I like to ask myself whether I'm committed or comfortable. Committed people grow and make an impact on the world around them. Comfortable people become complacent, dated, and disinterested in making the world around them a better place. Warning: if a vehicle is negatively affecting your health then that is a warning sign that you may be in an opportunity that is over your head. In that situation, you should speak to a mentor and/or seek professional help. I have been there more than once in my life and had to make course corrections with the help of mentors and professionals. My warning signs are ulcers, severe back problems, insomnia, and migraine headaches. Do you know your warning signs?

These three questions—Where is your final destination? Where is your next stop? And do you know how to operate this vehicle just enough not to crash it?—will keep you from getting lost on rabbit trails. What's a rabbit trail? I live in western Massachusetts, and I've never seen more rabbits before in my life! They are everywhere, and sometimes when I come out of the house early in the morning on my way to the gym and it's still dark, I'll hear some rustling in the leaves and it spooks me. I'll turn quickly to see a rabbit scurrying away. Rabbits have no sense of paths and sidewalks. Their philosophy in life is, "Any direction will do as long as I can find some good food to eat there."

People interested in learning how to use their gift to serve others and be well-compensated in the process cannot afford that philosophy in life. We must know our final destination and the best path to get there. There will be accidents and negative incidents in the way that cause us to take occasional detours. But once we get around those problems we get back on the path and take the best route to our destination. So, keep asking yourself, "What's my goal and final destination?" and it will keep you off rabbit trails and in the most appropriate vehicle for you, whatever stage of the journey you are in.

Another benefit of asking these questions is that it will keep you from trying to keep up with the Joneses. You don't need to keep looking over your shoulder or across the fence at what your college teammate or your neighbors are doing. You are all on different journeys that most often will require different vehicles. You don't want to be driving a Porsche when your journey requires you to go off-road. You don't want to be driving in an off-road Land Rover when this stage of your journey is on a freeway with a seventy-mile-an-hour speed limit. You want to be in the best vehicle for where you are in your journey. Have you ever asked yourself the question, "Do I know where I am going and am I driving the right vehicle?"

Let me give another example from sports. I grew up playing soccer, ice hockey, and lacrosse. I loved all three of these sports and took them as seriously as one can in high school. I did not lift weights back then, but I did other conditioning drills to get ready for each of the seasons. Each sport had different movements that one had to master to excel in it. Similarly, each vehicle requires a different skill set, and that's why you don't want to be focusing on what others are doing who are not in your field. I can tell you that my life as a teacher, coach, and author requires specific sacrifices and skills, and there is no sense comparing my vehicle with that of my neighbor across the street who sells real estate. What he drives, what he wears, and where he lives in many ways are determined by his gift and the vehicle that he's driving. So, there is no sense trying to live, dress, and drive like he does.

## Do the Research

Take some time to reflect on the best vehicle for you today. Who is someone in your field with whom you can talk and learn more about the vehicles they have driven over the course of their professional life? What kind of vehicles do you want to drive over the next five to ten years? If you can't obtain an apprenticeship or internship in a particular field, reading, watching, and listening about it is the next best thing. I'll give you the example of what I'm currently going through with doing webinars for the first time. I have listened to podcasts on this topic, particularly by Lewis Howes who has expertise in this areas. He has a related, how-to podcast that I have listened to several times. I listen to it, take notes, listen some more, take notes, apply what he says, and keep moving forward a little bit at a time.

Lewis Howes is a busy guy but I have access to him via podcast and videos, and you better believe I'm going to make the most of them. I do the same with gleanings from Dave Ramsey's podcast. He learned how to produce books that stay on bestselling book lists. Perhaps I'll get to meet him one day, but in the meantime, anything he writes or says about bookselling I'm going to consume several times plus take notes. This is what I mean by doing your research. Create your own independent study course and learn as much as you can from the sources that are available. If you have the opportunity to call an expert, do that, too! Glean as much as you can without being a nuisance.

Often people ask me how I do X, Y, or Z. When I've talked about it on a podcast, I share a link with them, as well as other content that will answer their questions. Ask yourself if you have acquired everything out there on the topic you want to learn more about in the career in which you think is right for your gift. I often find this when working with students on research projects. I read their rough draft, and when it's clear that they haven't done the necessary research, I let them know. When they tell me they couldn't find anything on the topic, my response is, "Why didn't you come to me? I told you at beginning of the semester that I am your mechanic and I'm here to help you fix what's not working. Plus, we have other mechanics at our campus library called reference librarians." Be sure that you are exhausting every available resource before you claim you've done your homework. There's nothing more impressive than someone who comes up to you to inquire about your area of expertise and has done their homework. When I run across people like that I'm excited about sharing what I know outside of the research that they've already done. However, I am less excited about talking with people when it's clear they haven't been diligent in doing their research.

## Vocational Callings

In his book *48 Days to the Work You Love,* Dan Miller says that a calling is something you learn to hear from your Creator. It's something that takes time and experience in which to tune your ear. For example, a professional mechanic can listen to the sound of an engine and diagnose a problem with a car that the amateur cannot hear. After reading this book, you will become sensitive to the ways God is calling you to use your gift. It's almost like somebody gives you hearing aids or a new pair of glasses that allows you to see the previously unseen.

The same is true when we decide to purchase something, especially a car. Once we decide what we want, we begin to see it everywhere. It isn't because the sales of the car have suddenly spiked and everyone is buying one. Instead, we have chosen to focus on that car and now have the ability to notice it. I think callings are the same way. God wants you to listen for the still and quiet voice that he uses daily to teach you more about who you are and what he's created you to do with the gifts he's given you. Some of us are just too busy multitasking to get quiet enough to hear the voice.

Some people have a sensitivity to small rattling sounds. When they get into a car, they immediately notice sounds that the rest of us cannot hear. When everybody stops talking and we turn off the podcast or music, we will all begin to hear a small rattling sound. It could be something like a small container in the side pocket of a car door on the passenger side. That's how God will speak to you if you get quiet enough and turn off enough of the activity in your life to hear Him. He's talking to you—you just have to get quiet enough to hear.

Now, some of you may think that I'm calling you to get in a monk's kneeling position in prayer. Not necessarily, although that may not be a bad idea. Everybody's different, but let me share some ways in which some are more attuned to the voice of God than others. For me, it's…when I go for a run in the morning…while walking in nature…while reading scripture… while reading books on the topic of gifts and callings…while sitting in church listening to a message. Have you ever gotten the feeling that God sent your mail to the person delivering the message that morning? Recall that feeling: *Somebody was reading my mail.* That's right. A message will come across that speaks directly to what you need to hear about who you are and how to use your gift. It's up to you to listen and act on it or not.

Most of us have the experience of growing up in neighborhoods in which we played all day until we heard, way off in the distance, our mom calling our name. It's like those dog whistles that are set to the frequency only dogs can hear. In the same way, God knows your frequency and he has been trying to get your attention in many different ways.

## A Fail-Safe Principle

There's a fail-safe principle that you can use to determine if it's God speaking to you. Just like your earthly father, God would only give you a gift that would make him look good. That's what the expression "to the glory of God" means—simply doing something that makes God look good. If you are engaged in something that makes God look good, you can be assured that you're hearing clearly, or, as I like to say, if it's legal, moral, and not fattening (see Romans 4:17-21).

> **Manuel Cuevas:** A native of Coalcomán, Mexico, Manuel Cuevas's older brother Adolfo, a tailor in Coalcomán, taught him how to sew at age seven. In one day, he made a shirt and a pair of pants for himself. He also made a suit for his First Communion. He recalls, "The guys at school were more about playing ball and the slingshots. That never interested me. I was really an outcast. I'd go to bed and I'd dream about fabrics and leathers and about the things that I'm going to make the next day." Cuevas had a gift for designing clothes and at an early age he accepted the calling to become a designer. He made a name for himself and today he is an icon in the music and fashion industry with his elaborate, rhinestone designs and embroidery. In the 1950s, he set up his business in Nashville, Tennessee. He would go on to design onstage garments for Hank Williams, Dolly Parton, and Johnny Cash. He goes on to say, "I've always done only one piece. I don't want to make two of anything. That's why I don't make socks. So, it's like history written again every day." When asked if he ever thought about retiring, he said, "No, I don't. I don't believe in that. I'm enjoying life and people keep giving me checks for it. You know, if I was away from my shop, I probably wouldn't be able to last more than fifteen days. The sewing machine and the needle and the thimble, that's it for me, you know."[50]

Dan Miller says that the average job lasts two years and four months and most people will have as many as sixteen jobs in a lifetime. A job is an expression of your calling and it's a vehicle for using your gift and nothing more. There are indicators that you have clearly understood your calling and you're in the right job. Here are some of them:

1.  First, you're like a fish in water when it comes to executing the essential skill. Fish are not taught to swim; like the Nike slogan, *they just do it*. Similarly, you just do it.
2.  Second, you find the process exhilarating and fulfilling.
3.  Third, you're naturally inclined to do it even if you aren't being compensated for it.

A student in a class I taught while writing this book shared that she had a gift for baking. She would bake all kinds of items to share with friends and family because she enjoyed doing it. It's what she did when she had extra time, something she found relaxing and enjoyable. I've seen her creations on her Instagram page. The girl has skills! But it took other people to explain to her that she's gifted in this area. It's quite common that gifted people assume that others can do the same thing they do, and that's why they don't think it's a gift. It's often our friends and family who point out that what we do so well is not normal for most people but a special gift. A gift results in joy and fulfillment in the work you do and that's one of the reasons you don't need to be compensated. It doesn't mean it's going to be easy, but it will bring you joy and fulfillment. And remember: if it's a calling it should complement your gift, which is something you can do better than anybody else with very little effort.

Let's also talk about the importance of dreams versus goals as you think about the next vehicle you want to drive associated with your calling. A goal is a dream with a timeframe for action attached to it. If you can't write it down on paper, then it's not a dream.

## Compensation

Here are some words of wisdom about compensation. As you upgrade vehicles, you should be upgrading in compensation as well. If not, you're going backward instead of forward. Also, know that compensation is a fluid concept that could be negotiated in most any situation. But first you must believe that you are the most gifted and best-prepared person for the position. A satisfying job is one in which you can use your gift to serve others and, in the process, you receive enjoyment, satisfaction, and earn a living. (We'll discuss more about compensation later in this chapter.) In his book *Simplify*, Bill Hybels says there are three ways you will know that you are in the right vehicle:

1. **Energy:** A rewarding job leaves you energized when you're serving others and it boosts your energy in the process. Being at work refills you. You naturally stay positive, because it's a positive situation and you are doing a task you enjoy with people you enjoy being around.

2. **Peace:** Take a job in a healthy culture in which roles are well-defined, directions are clear, and responsibilities are given with the authority to carry them out. This type of work environment is peaceful and energy is focused on doing the actual work. In that environment, people are free to excel in what they do best. The workday is simplified and your time spent outside work is also simplified. When you're at peace, others around you will sense it as well.

3. **Self-confidence:** A job you love boosts your self-esteem. You get to do things that God has gifted you to do. Progress gives you joy and makes you want to do more. You know you're making a difference and you are compensated accordingly—financially and with increased responsibilities. The ability to contribute causes one to feel great, like you do when you go for a great run or watch your team succeed in an athletic competition. It's a job that enables you to become a better you.[51]

## Job Alignment

How do you find a job that you will love so much that it simplifies your life? Hybels says make your choice based on four alignments: passion, culture, challenge, and compensation. We'll talk about each one of these below and the importance they play in determining the right fit for you and your gift. I want you to think about these four alignments as one turn of four on a combination lock, like the silver and black ones we used for the first time in middle school. The combination lock will not open unless each part of the combination is used. Similarly, the right fit for you in terms of a job needs to have almost equal parts that give you a fulfilling experience.[52]

## *Passion*

God hardwired everyone with a passion. For example, God gave me a passion for teaching. That passion gives me a love for teaching just about anything, so long as I'm teaching. I'm like a sponge full of water, but instead I'm full of teaching. If you just rub against me, teaching comes squirting out. As you can imagine, when my passion is pushed to the extreme it can get on folks' nerves. Just ask my former teammates.

Teaching is my primary passion but, like many of you, I also have secondary passions. For example, I'm passionate about cooking, financial stewardship, child rearing, and dressing and maintaining God's kingdom, which some folks today call environmentalism. What about you—what are you passionate about? What are those topics and issues in life that make your eyebrows go up, that give you a rush of adrenaline, that make you stand and deliver? In the process of teaching my students how to take notes, I teach them the cues that I show nonverbally when I'm speaking about something that they should be sure to note because it's more likely to show up on their exam. These are aspects of the content I'm passionate about that my students can see in my body language—in the veins that pop out on my head, in my voice inflection change, and when I become animated talking about them. Similarly, you respond when you're talking about your passion. A great book on the subject is *Let Your Life Speak: Listening for the Voice of Vocation* by Parker J. Palmer.

## *Culture*

You must find the right vocation in the right space to do what you need to ask the right questions. What is the company's climate and culture? How does the culture of the company fit with your personality and priorities? A good way to find out this information is to talk offline with an employee who has worked at the company for a few years. Before applying for a job, I have, over the years, tapped into my network and found out who is seven degrees of separation from somebody within the company in which I'm considering working. As a lacrosse player, I'm part of a close-knit fraternity, with members of our community working in just about every sector of society. Most often, I am a couple of phone calls and/or emails away from the right person to connect with to find out more about the company. Likewise, you should have a network that you could tap into—people who think like you and are glad to share what they know with you. A little bit of detective work can save you a lot of heartache. In the process, you also will have somebody to champion your application on the inside if you desire to move forward with seeking a job at a particular company. Is this a place where you can thrive? Is this going to be a good fit for you in terms of work-life balance? Do you and the company you're about to join share similar values? Is this company the right place for you to make a contribution? Will your work complement that of others at the organization?

### *Rigorous But Not Ridiculous*

When you do your best work, are you properly challenged or dangerously overchallenged? Operating at the optimal challenge level will bring you the most satisfaction. Everybody's different. You need to think about what is optimal for you, because what is optimal for you is different from what is optimal for me. Some people like working on several projects at the same time. Some people love to start new projects while others like to finish the work. A construction company usually has several types of workers—those who specialize in framing, others in sheetrock and taping, others in doing the finish work. All phases of construction are important, but they are not done equally well by all members of the team. You want to put yourself in a work scenario that optimizes your gift and personality.

Look at each challenge level. Underchallenged is when you are not adequately challenged to find what you are doing satisfying. For example, when I'm exercising I can tell if I'm working hard or not. When I'm not working hard enough to result in the type of fitness I'm after, I become discouraged from continuing to work out. By the way, that's why some folks don't work out. They go through the motions, don't work up a good sweat, and know that they're wasting their time. I would not describe myself as a runner, but I know it's the best way for me to drop weight because I'm sweating like a bandit! And by running regularly, I've developed a good habit—appropriate weight loss and fitness and ultimately great health and productivity.

It's the same thing with our work. In the field of exercise physiology, there is a term called atrophy. It explains what happens when you don't use a muscle: it becomes smaller and weaker. Similarly, when you're in a job that doesn't challenge your gift's talents and abilities they begin to go to waste and shrivel up. You want a job that provides a challenge that helps your gift's talents and abilities grow and get stronger and more effective. Remember the phrase "use it or lose it" when you're looking for a job.

I started learning Spanish in graduate school because part of the degree requirements included research proficiency in a foreign language; for historians, it's helpful to be able to read documents in more than one's native language. In my case, I developed a love of the Spanish language and wanted to do more than just pass the exam and move on. Postgraduate students take that approach; they learn enough to pass the exam and then never use the language skills again. To keep up my language skills, in graduate school I put myself in spaces where I could use and improve my Spanish speaking, listening, and writing skills. In the early days, I watched shows in Spanish for toddlers. To grow, I had to move on to more difficult levels, such as programming for middle school, then high school, then college.

Likewise, you don't want to stay in the same job if there's no room for advancement or opportunities that will force you to get better and better. Seek those opportunities that challenge you appropriately and make you grow professionally. Opportunities that challenge you force you to be sharper. One of the things I like about teaching at the college level is that I'm surrounded by students on the cutting edge of new technologies for developing and distributing content. These days, people understand that in the multimedia space content is king.

The bulk of the time I've spent writing this book I was in my second season of hosting two podcasts, one on food and one on sports. My producer and I had no idea how many people were listening to the podcast. My producer suggested we spend time understanding how to track our listeners, and that required consulting with somebody who understands website optimization and Google analytics. I talked to a colleague who suggested some undergrads who had developed expertise in these two fields. The students met with my producer and me and looked at our platforms, including my personal website, FredOpie.com. The students took one look at the website and challenged me to do better. It took us several weeks but we overhauled the site. It was a lot of work in addition to my responsibilities as a professor and author, but the exercise was a great example of work that challenged me appropriately and, in the process, energized me. It forced me to become more focused on what content *The Fred Opie Show* should showcase. It forced me to cut out the fat and stop wasting time on things that had nothing to do with my mission statement. You want to be at a job that forces you to get better and to let go of things that are a waste of time for your career goals, aspirations, and gifts. That's a great job setting and you should run to it!

Here's yet another example. I have a reputation as a professor who teaches rigorous courses. While writing this book, I was in my sixth year at Babson College. I've been at Babson long enough to see that the intermediate history courses I teach are filled with students who have come to the class with the expectation of a rigorous class, which they want, knowing it will make them better in the end. Students looking for an easy A don't take my courses. At the end of the process, the majority are grateful that they took the course because of the amount of information they learned and new skills they acquired. I run into former students on campus who had me in their first or second year and they'll greet me with a smile and a comment like: "I enjoyed the class I took with you; it's been one of my favorites so far." That's how you want your job to be—in a place that is rigorous but not ridiculous in its demands on your gift's talents and abilities.

Another characteristic of a job that challenges you appropriately is one in which you need to constantly seek the help and support of your coworkers. It forces everyone on the job to give maximum effort and to lean on one another for the collective good, which should be providing a service for others and in the process earning a good income. If you can use your gift's talents and abilities on your job and don't need help from others, over time you're going to become bored and your gift is going to atrophy. You'd better move on to a more challenging job before you lose proficiency in using it.

## Dangerously Overchallenged

Working in an overly challenging job is not fulfilling and it leads to burnout. Before long, something is going to give. It could be the death of your passion, stress on your home life, or the destruction of your health. I've heard of stories of people whose job became all-consuming in a destructive way. You've seen them, too: they look haggard and unkempt, and they're constantly fighting nagging colds and other sickness. When I am in a dangerously challenging situation my body begins to produce cold sores in my mouth. It's a way of my body telling me, "You'd better make an adjustment and make it quick."

I'm not talking about periods in which you have to put in additional hours and work to meet a deadline. That should happen occasionally on any job. But prolonged days of twenty-plus hours, eating on the go, running to put out one fire after the other on the job—those are all symptoms that you are in a dangerously challenging workspace and you need to get out. It's a toxic environment, and it won't be long before the toxins destroy your soul, which is made up of your mind, will, and emotions. It's in spaces like this that you find yourself slipping up ethically and doing things you never would've done before. It's a setting in which people may become more prone to marital and financial infidelity. A toxic workplace can also destroy you physically; it can really take away your good health.

## Appropriately Challenged-Plus

We do our best work in just-above appropriately challenging situations. We're talking about work in which you need to depend on God and colleagues and give your best effort in the process of serving others and making an income. You're in a situation in which you cannot cruise but instead have to paddle hard and steadily to keep up with others in your field. As a former athlete, I dedicate time daily to work on my book project. Why? Because I know I will get ahead if my competitors take a day off. When I still competed athletically I trained (ran and lifted weights) knowing that I would come out ahead of my opponents who chilled that day and relaxed. It wasn't about trying to hit home runs every day but instead being like George Brett, the Kansas City Royals Hall of Famer who focused on making contact and not on hitting home runs every time he stepped in the batter's box. By focusing on making contact with the ball, he hit home runs and lots of base hits, including singles, doubles, and triples. Having the right focus is what put him in position to be inducted into the Baseball Hall of Fame. Similarly, if you focus on doing the right things every day in your field instead of trying to be an overnight success, the opportunities of a lifetime to serve others with your gift will come your way.

Working in an appropriately challenged-plus job situation is similar to the feeling you get when you're having a great workout with weights and/or running. You get that burning sensation that's hard to push through but not impossible. It's the sensation you get when you know you're making progress, getting stronger, increasing your endurance, getting faster, burning that fat off, developing that six-pack, getting ripped! It's the sweet spot you hit when you're in the zone and you know you're working hard and accomplishing a lot. When you're in that place, your work satisfaction will be off the charts! It forces you to bring your A-game and leave it all at work, and when work is over you feel satisfied because you know you made an important contribution and you got better in the process. It's a job that requires you to leave it all on the field.

Whose job is it to get you to that level at work? Who should be making the adjustments so that you're working in that appropriately challenged-plus scenario? That's your job. You need to make the adjustments. It may require changing to a new vehicle because this one has run its course and you've mastered everything you can master on it.

I'll never forget when I made the transition from a master's program to a doctorate program in history. From the first day of classes, I realized I would have to bring my A-game-plus. In one of my classes I had to read these enormous books, many of them over four-hundred pages. We had one week to read the book and provide a one-page, double-spaced book review that we would have to distribute to the entire class and the professor. I had never done anything like that before, and it took all I had in me to get it done on time. On more occasions than I want to admit, I would be completing the assignment just before the start of class and sprinting to class to make it on time. The feeling of failure surrounded me.

But over time I learned the strategies necessary to read and comprehend the material faster, and my typing skills improved drastically, which allowed me to get the assignments in on time. Keep in mind that when I entered graduate school I had never used a computer before and I didn't know how to type. So, each and every step of the graduate school process was an appropriately challenging-plus scenario. But each time the work challenged me to get better and work harder and smarter, I did. There were times when I didn't think I was cut out for the work, but eventually I learned a new process and I leaned on my classmates and those ahead of me in the doctoral program to get better. By the end of the first year, I started to gain some traction and felt better about my intellectual abilities.

I spoke to my master's degree graduate school advisor Dr. Hughes at Shippensburg University, where I earned my master's degree in history. I asked her why she didn't tell me the work at the doctoral level would be so hard. She responded, "I couldn't tell you because it was something you would have to go through and figure out on your own. However, I knew you were the kind of student who would rise to the level of the competition, and I was sure that if you worked as hard as you did with me you would have a hard time at first, make the necessary adjustments, and thrive."

I remember my first professorship at Morehouse College in Atlanta. I had taught many times before, but this was the first time as a history professor managing my own class, creating syllabi, exams, and so on. At first it seemed like a daunting task. I was wise enough to lean on my mentors and ask colleagues as I tried to figure out how to do my job as an assistant professor of history. Just as I learned the first year in my doctoral program, the first year as an assistant professor was hard, but I learned, made mistakes, gave it my best effort, and developed my chops as a professor. Later I went up for tenure, which frankly scares the daylights out of many academics because it's not a sure thing at all. But I learned the process and managed to go through it without a lot of fear because I knew what I had to do and I brought my A-game.

The same could be said of publishing my first book. That was a daunting, more than an appropriately challenging situation. I submitted the book to something like fifteen publishers and I received rejection letters from them all. Again, I leaned on colleagues who had gone through the process themselves. Getting my first books published forced me to use my best effort and it made me grow as a scholar. There were so many different aspects of research, writing, editing, and learning how to find appropriate artwork for the book and then getting the rights to publish it from the owners of the images. There were so many new things I had to learn, and indeed it was a challenging process. But I recently published book number five and I have the process down to a science. What used to take me five years to do I can now do in half the time. Additionally, I can teach the steps to others because I made so many mistakes the first several times I submitted a book for publication.

There is no doubt that an appropriately challenging-plus work situation is rewarding and makes you grow. It's the one you want to be in even when you are working harder than you want to. The results are so rewarding. I'll never forget when my first book came out and my publisher sent me copies. I opened the box of books in front of my wife and our toddlers, Kennedy and Chase. I raised the box of books over my head and we marched around the house with me in front and them following and cheering. While writing this chapter, copies of my most recent book, the fifth one, arrived at my house just before Thanksgiving. My mother-in-law had flown in for the holiday and I had the opportunity to open the box of books in front of her. It's an amazing experience to see something that you worked on for months come to fruition. It's a very satisfying feeling. I've never run a marathon, but I imagine it must be similar to the feeling one has after training for months for the Boston Marathon and finally crossing the finish line with a triumphant "I did it!" Finding the right challenge at work is like tuning your engine. Driving a car with the engine tuned is a whole lot more fun than driving one that is clinking and clanking as you go down the road.

## *More on Compensation*

Scriptures tells us that the worker is worthy of his wages. Compensation differs across professions, years of experience, and regions. But don't get caught up in compensation alone. There is a whole lot to be said about the importance of job satisfaction and performing work you're passionate about.

There's also the question of the commute. After graduating from college, I took a teaching job in Danbury, Connecticut, as I mentioned earlier. To save money and pay expenses such as student loan debt, I lived at home with my parents and paid them rent. It also meant I drove to work fifty minutes each way, five days a week. That commute left an indelible mark on my decision-making process. There were times when I was so tired that when I pulled into the driveway it startled me because I didn't remember most of the trip; I felt like I drove home asleep. It's scary to think about how many people injure themselves or someone else because of falling asleep at the wheel.

About ten years later, I took a teaching job that required a seventy-five-minute commute, about sixty-five minutes on a commuter rail and a ten-minute bike ride from my home to the train station and then from the train station to campus. This commute proved far superior to the driving one, but if there was a problem with the kids it took a long time to get back home. My current gig is a twenty-minute commute, if that. It makes my life so much simpler. When I consider taking a job offer, the commute most definitely plays a role in the final decision. It's not just the length of the commute but also the cost of the commute and the cost of my time. So, it's not a deal-breaker, but it is something in which you need to count the cost, as the scriptures says.

I like the way Bill Hybels talks about compensation. He looks at the equation of pay versus passion. He advises us to compensate where compensation is needed on both sides of the spectrum. For example, if you're in a great-paying job that doesn't provide enough satisfaction in terms of using and exercising your gift to help others, then supplement it with a job and/or volunteer opportunity that provides the satisfaction component. Likewise, if you're in a job that provides great satisfaction in terms of exercising your gift and serving others but doesn't meet your financial needs, then compensate with extra work that does. I love that analogy. Too often we focus on our income while neglecting the need to have a job that is fulfilling and satisfying.

For example, I love my job as a college professor, but it doesn't satisfy me in terms of giving me the opportunity to teach the word of God, which is something I'm called to do and an area I'm gifted in. But I'm a member of a men's Bible study group that meets once a week and, more often than not, provides an opportunity for me to teach the word. It gets me pumped up and it serves the brothers in that group, who come ready to eat a great spiritual meal. Similarly, my job as a professor doesn't provide an outlet for me to satisfy my desire for coaching lacrosse and mentoring young men and women in the process. However, I'm a volunteer coach, which provides that opportunity for me. See what I mean? When my job as a professor doesn't meet my financial commitments, I supplement my income as a paid public speaker and receive royalties from the books I publish. The same is true when I serve on panels in which I share my expertise as a culinary historian.

Taking a page from Hybels, I view compensation like shopping for groceries. Here is a free plug for the places where I shop. The majority of what I need to stock my cupboards with I can find at four locations: Costco, Trader Joe's, Whole Foods, and a place called Russo's. If you think about it, most of you shop in multiple places because you don't have one place where you can get all your shopping needs met. However, for some reason, we think that our job should meet all our financial commitments and satisfy our desire to use our gift to serve others. That's a lot of expectation for one place, occupation, and/or employer. If you have a job that meets both of those needs, God bless you—stop complaining and get back to work!

On the question of pay, we get to the nitty-gritty. The Bible tells us that if we don't take care of our own we are worse than an infidel. What that means is that you can't afford a hobby—you need a job. A hobby is something that you do because you love it and you're passionate about it but it can't pay the bills. There are too many people who have dependents and yet are wasting valuable time consumed in hobbies without the ability to meet their financial responsibilities. You need to do some serious soul-searching and have a heart-to-heart with your mentor if you're in that situation. You need to get a job that meets your financial responsibilities and then carve out time in your schedule for your hobbies. Get your priorities in shape.

That was the case with me when I was still a competitive athlete. As I mentioned earlier, I spent a lot of time and way too much money invested in sports when I still had student loan debt. As Dave Ramsey often says, the best place to go when you're in debt is to work. When you're in debt you need to put your passion on hold and get out of debt so that you can move into the space of doing work you're passionate about that pays well or doing work you're passionate about but also another job that subsidizes your pay. I'm not saying that if you start a business you should be making millions off the bat. As the old saying goes, anything that is not growing is dead. And when you are in debt you cannot afford to be messing around with something that is not bringing in enough to meet your financial needs and get you out of debt ASAP. When you get yourself into a better financial situation, then you can ease yourself into another income-earning situation that satisfies your passion.

The flipside of this scenario is having a job that makes a good salary but does nothing to satisfy your passion and not having another way to subsidize that passion and make use of your gift. I know some people in this position. I'm not talking about a temporary situation to clean up your finances. I'm talking about getting a job that pays well and staying in it way too long and being seriously unsatisfied in the process, but rich. What's good about making big money and in the process you're out of control, have no peace, and you are an emotional wreck? (see Matthew 16:26) That's what it's like to be in a great-paying job that provides no satisfaction. You feel like you're losing your soul (mind, willpower, and emotional stability). You feel that way because that's exactly what you are doing when you're not using your gifts and abilities to serve others and get paid in the process. There may be many opportunities for you to make big money, but they provide little passion in return, and you're doing nothing to subsidize that job with something that *is* satisfying to you. So, yes, you need to make a change if you want to have peace.

When you position yourself to gain wealth devoid of a passion for what God has created you to do, you become spiritually bloated and joyless. The idea that you can't be compensated well for doing what God has created you to do is strictly a fallacy and is something rooted in leftist ideology without biblical literacy. God is looking for vessels through whom he can pour out his gifts and show his love and care to those in need. Do you want to be that kind of person?

Here's an anecdote that I think demonstrates a few points I'm making. Francis X. Kelly, Jr. (affectionately called BF for Big Frank) and his wife, Janet, started a small insurance company in the basement of their Timonium, Maryland, home in 1976. In addition to the business, BF and his wife have been engaged in public service and giving as part of their spiritual disciplines as Christians. They are the parents of four boys, and I came to know their oldest son, Frank III, at a summer lacrosse tournament in Glastonbury, Connecticut, a suburb of Hartford, in 1986. At the same time, Frank started working full-time in his family's business.

Frank was the first guy I had ever met in lacrosse who shared a similar spiritual journey to mine. At the Glastonbury tournament, he shared with me his vision of starting a lacrosse ministry. I told him I was all in. One year later, in the summer of 1987, Frank started the Fellowship of Christian Athletes (FCA) lacrosse ministry with seed money and support from his family's business. Frank would go on to organize the first annual FCA Lacrosse Camp at Gettysburg College, in which I participated on the all-volunteer coaching staff. We had about eight players, and several of them had been the children of football coaches volunteering at the FCA football camp and also at Gettysburg College.

These seven-to-ten-year-olds had never played lacrosse. The lacrosse camp provided childcare for the football coaches' kids. At the camp, I began a relationship with Gettysburg Men's Lacrosse Coach Hank Janczyk (Coach J) and the late national Lacrosse Hall of Famer Peter Kohn. (If you haven't seen the movie *Keeper of the Kohn*, do so ASAP!) My two children attended the FCA Lacrosse Camp at Gettysburg for the first time in 2009. The camp had more than four-hundred male and female players in attendance. Frank provided the vision and seed money and solicited the volunteers necessary to plan and expand FCA lacrosse. Over several decades, it has expanded and continues to expand across the country. Today, it's a dynamic ministry and a respected brand across the lacrosse community. People who don't know the core of its activities and goals—such as a relationship with Jesus Christ and with one's brothers and sisters via huddles (Bible study), prayer, worship, and retreats—view it as one of the top club lacrosse programs and brands in our game.

Today, Kelly & Associates Insurance Group is one of Maryland's fastest-growing privately held firms. It is the region's leading health insurance broker/administrator, with nearly 13,000 corporate clients and 450 employees. BF and Janet continue to model for their four boys and their families how to live like no one else so that you can contribute in multiple ways like no one else. As a family, they participate in numerous causes and ministries. They are one of the best examples of entrepreneurs in action that I know who get paid and satisfy their passions, which makes a positive difference in the lives of others.

I already told you about what my friend Frank has done for FCA Lacrosse. Frank played collegiate lacrosse and so did his brothers. His brother, John, runs the company's benefit strategies. He is passionate about cycling and rode as a member of the national USA Cycling team's Tour of

Mexico and Tour of Costa Rica events. John is an active board member of the Mount Washington Pediatric Hospital and serves as an elder and Bible teacher at Grace Fellowship Church in metropolitan Baltimore. Brother David is a member of the company's Executive Management Team. Outside of work, he is the President of the Board of the Dyslexia Tutoring Program, which helps children from low-income families overcome their reading difficulties. He also serves as a member of the board of directors of several nonprofit organizations, including a shock trauma center, schools, and scholarship funds. Frank's youngest brother, Bryan, is the president of KELLY Marketing Services, a division of KELLY. In addition to his responsibilities at KELLY, Bryan serves on the boards of several nonprofit organizations and ministries, including the Fellowship of Christian Athletes Maryland Lacrosse Club. Bryan is also a successful men's varsity lacrosse coach at the high school that he and his brothers all attended, Calvert Hall College High School in Baltimore. You can listen to interviews I did with the Kelly brothers on my podcast, *The Fred Opie Show*, which can be found on the podcast page on my website FredOpie.com. Discovering your gift and using it to serve others and make an income and a difference in the world is rewarding. A case study of how the Kellys have combined their work and their callings provides a living example that others can emulate.

I'm ending this chapter with a story about my father. My dad died of leukemia, a type of cancer, in 2008. While he was undergoing treatment in Sloan Kettering Hospital in New York City, I had the opportunity to do a recorded interview with him. I did the interview based on a book suggestion from Joe Ehrmann, whose work centers around the issue of authentic manhood and helping boys become men. One of the biggest challenges Joe talks about in his work is that men have a problem with releasing their feelings and sharing their inner life with each other. He suggests—and I do, too—that you read the book *Questions for My Father: Finding the Man Behind Your Dad* by Vincent Staniforth as a way of learning more about your dad. My dad was a member of that generation that didn't say much, remained stoic most of the time, and lived by the credo celebrated in the old E.F. Hutton commercials: don't say much, but when you do, make it something people want to hear.

As it relates to this chapter on finding the right job, I asked my father the question from the book: "What did you really want to be when you were a young man starting in the working world?" My father's response floored me. Let me first give you some context. At that point, my dad was a retired Sing Sing prison guard. It was his main gig, and he also operated a side business performing janitorial services for small businesses and some homes. This is what Dad said when I asked the question:

I wanted to be an attorney, and not just any attorney. I wanted to be like Thurgood Marshall, a civil rights attorney litigating cases against discrimination in front of the US Supreme Court. [Marshall was one of the leading civil rights attorneys for the NAACP that helped end Jim Crow segregation in North America. President Lyndon B. Johnson would later appoint Marshall as the nation's first African American Supreme Court judge.] I never pursued that dream because I had some kind of learning disability like dyslexia, something like you have, that I wasn't able to get around it. So, instead, I went into the Air Force, which I really enjoyed. I should've probably made a career out of it. I used the GI Bill to enroll in night school at Westchester County Community College. During the day, I worked full-time at the General Motors plant in North Tarrytown. My day job was exhausting, and before long I dropped out of school because I couldn't handle the demands of both school and that job. I met your mother and we got married quickly thereafter and had our first child [my older brother Randy]. I then took the civil service exam and landed the job at the prison, where I remained for more than twenty-five years. But yeah, I wanted to be an attorney.

I'll never forget my dad sharing that career aspiration and unfulfilled dream with me. I hope you never forget it either as you think about the best vehicles in which to use the gift/s that God gave you. If you want to be a lawyer and are telling yourself, "But going to law school will take three years of my life," consider this: If you don't go to law school it will still take three years of your life. As my mother used to say, time stops for no one. And since you know that, why not make the best of it and do the work that you find challenging and fulfilling?

# CHAPTER 6

# Live on a Monthly Budget and Have an Emergency Fund

While you're in the training stage of your life—whether you decided that you needed a college degree or to enroll in a vocational training program and/or apprenticeship—you need to live on a monthly budget. Dave Ramsey makes it easy with the free online budgeting system available as an app from the site everydollar.com. Folks, if I can do it, you can do it. And if you have a good income and very little to show for it, you need to start living on a monthly budget. Yup, I follow Dave's baby steps. I cut up my credit cards and live on cash and use debit cards.

Those in the training stage of life should have an emergency fund of $500 and stop all investing. The best investment you can make is in obtaining the training necessary for you to use your gift to serve others and make a great income in the process. If you've already accumulated debt to pay for your training, commit to not accumulating any further debt and going on a scorched earth monthly budget to cash-flow (budget and pay cash for) the rest of your training. I encourage you to read Dave's book, *The Total Money Makeover*, which has served as a template for this book. It will give you the baby steps to turn your financial situation around. We'll talk later in this chapter in more detail about the baby steps. But if you do have debt, these steps outlined in the *Total Money Makeover* can help you gain financial freedom and peace. Here are some essential steps you can take:

1. Commit to paying cash
2. Stop eating out
3. Stop going on vacation
4. Take an extra job and work overtime

In most instances, if you work like crazy for a short period of time, say six months to a year, you can clear up your debts and be in position to start building wealth using the plan laid out in the rest of this chapter.

The next step in your journey is to live on a monthly budget and save three to six months of living expenses as an emergency fund. I only recently learned this step and it has made all the difference in my life. If I had started this when I was in college I would have been a multimillionaire before the age of forty.

My father taught me the value of hard work from a young age. I always had to hustle to make money. I worked with my brother delivering newspapers. I worked as a gofer in an artsy boutique in my hometown, emptying the garbage and breaking down boxes. I also stocked shelves at a grocery store, too. But my best-paying gig was working with my father on the weekends. As I mentioned, he operated a janitorial business on the weekend cleaning offices, a firehouse, and a church. I worked hard, mopping, vacuuming, cleaning toilets, emptying and cleaning ashtrays, and washing windows. My father paid me probably more than I deserved, allowing me to always have cash on hand. The same was true when I got into college and graduate school.

But the missing ingredient was that I never had a game plan for building wealth. When I started my Christian walk as a junior in college, I learned about the work of Ron Blue and Larry Burkett. Both had a calling to use their gift to teach people how to be good stewards of their money. I learned to hate debt and it became a practice for the rest of my life, but I failed to follow their game plan and other areas of financial stewardship. As a result, I made purchases I had no business making and I spent more on sports than I should have. During my undergraduate years, I had summer jobs, but instead of stockpiling the money to ensure that I would get through college without debt, I spent way too much on traveling to play in summer leagues and tournaments. For example, I lived up in Westchester County and would drive to Long Island to play in the old Freeport summer league and Cantiague Park league in Nassau County. The trip took about an hour to an hour and a half each way, depending on traffic. I drove a gas-gargling Chevrolet Caprice and had to pay some hefty tolls to cross the Throgs Neck and Whitestone bridges.

Yes, those summer leagues were fun and I got better playing in them, but in return they left me broke. I should've been saving a pile of cash to complete my undergraduate studies without taking out loans to pay for the various expenses one incurs going to college. If I had been on a monthly budget I could've decided better and probably could've afforded to play in summer leagues. But I had no plan and I was a financial accident, going no place, like many of you. If you can manage five dollars, you can manage $500 or $5,000. That's why most professional athletes go broke within a year after their career has ended.

Let me tell you about some of the stupid things I did after I became educated and had a college degree. As my mother would say, there's nothing worse than an educated fool—and financially, that's what I was. Upon receipt of my first teaching job, I was normal. I went to an Acura dealership and bought a new car with a car loan and zero down. I took the first step in squandering the most important financial tool I had—my income. One day I was listening to Ron Blue or Larry Burkett on the radio talk about the scripture that says the borrower is the slave of the lender. What he said stopped me in my tracks. I took the steps to sell the new car and purchased a very good, used Honda Prelude with low mileage. This step got me out of debt and I went on to ride that Honda from 1986 until I got married in 2000. Think about how much money I saved in car payments. Let's say that the car loan on the new Acura had been $200 a month. Two hundred dollars a month over ten years invested in mutual funds with a 10 percent return would have made me a very wealthy thirty-two year old. When I put it like that it makes you think, doesn't it?

Let's talk about some of the stupid things I did in my post-collegiate years. Before the advent of professional major league lacrosse in the United States, the best players played club ball and the best of the best had the goal of making a national team. I played in two national championships as a Syracuse player. Following my senior year, I took a year off from playing, feeling burnt out. But in 1986 I decided to try out for the 1990 US national team. To make that team, you had to play well enough to earn an invitation to try out in the summer of 1989. I held the view that playing for a great club team would put me in position to earn a tryout. In 1986, I lived at home with my parents in Westchester County and commuted to Danbury, Connecticut, where I worked as a public schoolteacher. For two years, I commuted fifty minutes to work every day, as I related earlier, and then in the spring I would commute almost ninety minutes to Nassau County,

Long Island, to play for Long Island lacrosse club. Imagine: my teammates and I paid to play, and we played with great passion. Most of the guys on the team lived on the island, but not me, which made playing for the team an expensive proposition that ate up my teacher's salary.

Let me be more specific about my stupidity. I traveled twice a week as a broke guy! Translation: I had debt in school loans and should've focused on paying them off. Instead, I made road trips in the spring for two years twice a week to Long Island for practice and games. I also played in summer tournaments that required the expense of travel and lodging at venues in New England and as far away as Vail, Colorado.

In 1988, I took a job teaching in the Hempstead public school system and relocated to the same town that served as the base for my club team. That winter I tried out and made the New York Saints professional indoor lacrosse team. At the time, we played in the Nassau Coliseum. I should say my teammates played in the Nassau Coliseum, because I dressed for two away games out of a sixteen-game schedule. The pay was lousy and if I did the math it didn't cover the commute to practice and how much time I invested in staying in shape to play sixteen games. I chalk that season up to what Dave likes to call the stupid tax—the price you pay when you make decisions without good mentors in your life and you become so hell-bent on doing something that it's like having a fever. Some people have house fever: no matter what you tell them about the proper way to purchase a home, they can't hear you. We will turn to that topic shortly because I paid some stupid tax in that regard as well.

In the summer of 1989, I received an invitation to try out for the 1990 US men's national team but had no money to cover the expenses involved. But no, I didn't think about that. It's only now that I've been cured of the fever I had for lacrosse that I can say I was thrilled to get the tryout, though I was still broke and paying off student loans. When the tryouts for the USA team came in 1989 I had to foot the bill to travel twice to Rutgers University in New Brunswick, New Jersey, where they were held. Things have changed with the US national team experience for players, but in those days the players had to either do some serious fundraising or cut a check to be a member of the team. The 1990 World Lacrosse Cup was held in Australia, which is not a short or inexpensive trip. I'm not ungrateful for the opportunity. I'm just kicking myself in the butt for being so stupid, fiscally speaking. I made the team, and when I returned from the games I moved to Gettysburg to begin working at Gettysburg College and getting a master's in history at Shippensburg University. I still had student loans and my financial situation could best be described as precarious for a first year graduate student and assistant lacrosse coach going to school at night. I left the Long Island lacrosse club to become a member of our archrival, Maryland Lacrosse Club, based in Baltimore. Like my experience back in New York, I would commute twice a week for about an hour each time from Gettysburg to Baltimore for games and practices.

I played for the club for two years while attending graduate school, which had been another roughly one-hour commute twice a week in my (thank God) fuel-efficient Honda Prelude. I miss that old car. In my last year at Gettysburg I worked as an interim dean, making serious money, which allowed me to pay off my student loan and have an emergency fund. In the spring of 1992, Maryland Lacrosse Club had a great season and we advanced to the club championship on Long Island in New York. But I had a problem. I had just been accepted to the graduate program in history at Syracuse University, and to get ready for the foreign-language exam, I registered for an immersion program in Guadalajara, Mexico. I was so lacrosse insane that I went to Mexico and committed to my club team to return for the club championship game. In retrospect, it sounds crazy!

I got off a long and tiring flight from Mexico to New York, sleepy as all get out, and headed straight to my folks' house in Croton to pick up my car and equipment, which required driving ninety minutes north, packing everything up, and then turning around and driving another ninety minutes to the game. I made it to the game with barely enough time to warm up before the start of the opening faceoff. In the final analysis, we won the club championship, but my club team manager reneged on his commitment to pay for my travel back and forth, and there went my emergency fund to pay the expenses. It left me returning to Mexico and entering a graduate program later that fall with no emergency fund. It took me a long time to recover from that stupid decision and it made my experience and graduate school much tougher than it needed to be because I didn't have a budget or backup plan.

I'm glad I stopped playing before the club team and showcase tournament scene started. Parents are spending between $3,000 to $5,000 to be on a club and on average $10,000 to travel and play in three or more tournaments every year during middle and high school. These are people who are broke. Remember my definition of broke: you have consumer debt other than a home mortgage, such as car loans, student loans, and credit card debt. Before you laugh at me, which you should, think about what you're fanatical about and how much you spend on it. There's nothing wrong with recreational activities and hobbies when you plan and budget for them, but I had no plan. I put stuff on my credit card and worked extra jobs all for the love of the game. Sounds good, but it was stupid!

I got married in 2000 and we had our first child in 2002. Let me share the dumb decision that we made as a new married couple and young parents. Everybody tells you when you get married that you've got to buy a house. It's a good investment. But it's not a good investment when you're broke and you can't afford a down payment or have three to six months of living expenses for emergencies. We have just purchased our third home. The first two we had no business buying, because we did not have enough to put 20 percent down and avoid paying private mortgage insurance, we had no emergency savings, and we had some debt, largely student loan debt, to pay off. So, let me tell you what happens when you buy houses this way. Stupid and dumb come to live with you in your new home, and when you need to make a home repair or replace a broken appliance you're forced into making a poor decision and going further into debt. You can't enjoy the home because you're so stressed out and fearful of what might happen next that would drive you further into debt. We didn't do this once—we did this twice!

I describe financial stress as riding on bicycle tires that are supposed to have a maximum of fifty pounds of pressure that instead have seventy-five pounds of pressure. The least little financial mishap that happens in your life, such as a car repair or a health issue, leads to a blowout that throws you into an emergency and you have no emergency funds to fix it. One of Dave's steps to financial peace calls for building an emergency fund of three to six months of living expenses. That takes the financial pressure out of your bike tires, and as a result, a bump doesn't lead to a blowout emergency because you have an emergency fund for situations that arise. I call it being your own banker.

Let me caution you: Clearly define what is something that should be a category in your monthly budget versus an emergency. For example, I have car that I have owned for more than five years. On average, when it goes into the shop for regular maintenance or an unexpected repair, it costs us about $400, so I have an auto category as part of my monthly budget that includes $400. If we don't use it in a month, cool—but if I need it there's no panic and I can pay for the repair without freaking out.

My experience financially had been living paycheck to paycheck and putting out one fire after another and repairing one blowout after another for too long. From the outside, no one could tell just how bad my financial situation was. And that's the case with most of the people around us; they are suffering from a lack of financial peace. Just like a sponge full of water, if anything squeezes them just a bit, such as a relationship problem at home or on the job, they lose their cool and the real person comes out. Their financial situation has them hurting, and, as I have observed, hurt people hurt people. Have I convinced you yet of the importance of living on a monthly budget and having three to six months of emergency savings in the bank? This is a good time to share this piece of wisdom: The time to fix your roof is when it's nice and sunny out. Once the rain starts it's really hard and dangerous to get up on a wet roof and repair it. And if you're going to hire somebody, believe me, people in the roofing business get busy during storms, so why not call them when the weather's nice?

The one thing that I wish I had known was just how important it is for you to determine where you want your money to go instead of your money telling you where to go. I became extremely frustrated because I had a good-paying job but I still lived paycheck to paycheck. I started listening to the podcast of *The Dave Ramsey Show*. If you've never heard of Dave Ramsey, you're probably living like I did for too many years. What happened was that I downloaded an NPR app that gave me access to all kinds of podcasts. I've always been very active and enjoyed listening to public radio talk shows as I go about the mundane things of life, such as working out and commuting to work. So, one day I'm looking for more stuff to listen to. I'd heard of Dave Ramsey earlier in life but didn't know much about him. I found this app of his show and decided to check it out. Dave does a daily, three-hour show that he makes available as a podcast as well as on YouTube.

I started downloading the show and consuming it like hot biscuits with butter and strawberry jam! I started learning why I was living paycheck to paycheck despite having a great income. The first problem was that I had no monthly budget. I now have what Dave calls a zero-dollar budget, in which you take your paycheck and assign every bit of it to a category that you decide. To be frank, I been doing it for about a year and a half. My finances have completely turned around. I stopped making stupid decisions with my money, and as a result my finances turned around for good. The process of working on the monthly budget takes perhaps thirty minutes once you get the system down. When I first started doing a monthly budget it was ugly, nasty, and stressful. But it's getting better every day as I get my reps putting together a monthly budget.

Now, some of you who are what Dave calls free spirits are starting to get anxious already because you don't want to get boxed in. A budget sounds like claustrophobia. It's not true. A budget gives us the freedom to spend money. What do I mean by that?

Once I have taken care of life's most important responsibilities—food, shelter, and utilities—I then move on to making wise choices with my money. I save, invest, and give. I want to be sure I have three to six months' emergency savings and that I am investing my money for retirement. As an evangelical Christian, I practice the discipline of giving a minimum of 10 percent of what I make. After that, the remaining monthly income that I receive I put toward lifestyle choices. These are choices such as the type of shelter that I rent or purchase, the type of transportation I use to get from point A to point B, the type of clothing I decide to wear, the type of hairstyle and grooming I decide on, the type of food I choose to purchase, the amount of eating out I choose to do, and how much travel I decide to participate in.

When I designate my money I have the freedom to spend so long as I can pay for it in cash. For example, I love to shop at thrift stores. I know it may sound strange to some of you, but don't knock it until you try it! I find it relaxing. Similarly, I enjoy cooking and baking; it's something else I find relaxing. I also enjoy recreational activities, such as traveling, skating, running, and biking. I can do these without feeling guilty about any of them so long as I have taken care of the most important responsibilities first and then made wise decisions in terms of saving, investing, and giving.

I use Dave Ramsey's envelope system for our cash categories and a debit card for other expenses, most of which I've set up as a direct payment system that pays bills like my housing cost and utilities automatically. I have envelopes for food, gas, toiletries, stationery, clothing, eating out, and my favorite category of all—Fred's fun money! Once I've spent the money in a particular envelope, that's it until the next payday. Or I look at my monthly budget and see where I may have over calculated. If that's the case, I decide to move the money over to another category or envelope. I have every dollar on my laptop and on my smartphone, so it's very easy to write down expenses and to move things around or check the category's balance status. I now have more money than I've ever had before, and I spend without feeling guilty.

# CHAPTER 7

# Live and Give Like No One Else

In this last chapter, I want to draw a picture of the life I am living and which I know thousands of others are living and inspiring me in the process. As I mentioned, I started using Dave Ramsey's seven baby steps. I had already found a job where I could use my gifts and ability to serve others and make a good income. But because I mismanaged my money I had little to show for it and the idea of giving to others in need was impossible.

Let me tell you about what's happened since understanding my gifts, having mentors in my life, obtaining the training needed to do my job, and having many years to develop the reps necessary and different types of jobs to live the way I'm living now. My life is not free of problems, but I now have the tools to move beyond constant pity parties every time things don't go the way I want them to go.

Living like no one else means having a calling and career rather than a job that just pays the bills. It's more than just being compensated well for what you do. It's about being excited about making a difference with your gifts and talents. I have a good friend from high school who makes a boatload of money. But he once told me that his dream job would be teaching history at the high school level. Now, before you start going off, this is what he said; it may not be your dream job but it is his. According to him, he is so committed financially to the nice house in the suburbs, kids in private school, and the lifestyle his family is wedded to that he can't walk away from his lucrative salary to do the thing that would make him feel fulfilled. So, that's part of my definition of living like no one else: having a fulfilled life.

Being normal is having a job that pays well and gives you security. But I ask you, is that what you want? Paid security for the next twenty-five to thirty years of a working career? Not me baby, no way. In the words of Zig Ziglar, when the opportunity clock goes off in the morning, 80 percent of the time I'm fired up to get out of bed. In fact, I'm so fired up that I'm awake by 4:00 a.m. I can't wait to get my groove on and make a difference! Just before I started to write this section of the book, I got an email from a student I taught last semester. He asked me if I could schedule some time to talk with him about something important he wanted to ask my advice about. I love that about my job! I teach semester after semester, student after student, and I'm more than a history teacher. I'm teaching history and, in the process, talking about life to young people who are at the stage of trying to figure out what their gifts and talents are and how they want to make a living. And I'm pouring into them examples of people throughout history who made an impact—negative and positive—on society.

At Babson College, we have one major only: business. Yes, we have concentrations in finance, accounting, and so on, but we teach business. When we first came to Babson as a couple to teach here, my wife being in the business part of our duo, I did wonder at first, what's a history professor going to do at a business school? Well, it didn't take me long to figure out that I had the God-given opportunity to help shape the business leaders of the future. And I would do everything in my power to make sure that we had socially responsible leaders who put ethics before income, who put concern for others before profit shares, and who thought about being good stewards of the environment when they decided on suppliers for what they produced. I asked my students to think about those questions so they can live and give like no other entrepreneurs have done before.

So, when my students contact me and say they want to talk, more often than not something I said in the course of the semester has stuck in their craw and it's bugging them and making them rethink what they want to do with their gifts and ability. You may think I'm an optimist, and if you do you're right. But I've been doing this for more than twenty years now and know the questions that will keep you from going to sleep at night if you're heading in the wrong direction. I consider it an honor and a privilege to be able to give students advice. Live like no one else and make an impact on the world around you.

Secondly, I talk in this chapter about the ability to give like no one else. It is the vision that I want you to get a hold of. It's the same one that I ran smack dab into when I started listening to Dave Ramsey's "millionaire theme hour," which he does every so often on his podcast. He puts the call out to folks who have a net worth of more than $1 million. That is when you add up what you own minus what you owe and it adds up to more than $1 million. Listening to these millionaire hours has inspired me. If you're anything like me, when you think of millionaires you think of people like the Kennedys of Boston or perhaps an entertainer or professional athlete. These are not the folks who call in to Dave's show. These are people who came from families with the same, if not less, wealth than mine. I'm the son of a Sing Sing prison guard who operated a janitorial service on the weekends with his three boys and who worked overtime at the prison four out of seven days most weeks of the year. I came from neither a rich nor a poor family.

The people who call the show have several things in common. They've worked hard as teachers, public servants, small business owners—folks with normal jobs. They've lived on less than they earned. Many of them buy their clothes like I do today, at thrift stores. They drove secondhand cars and lived in moderate homes in which they paid off their mortgage as soon as possible. They got on a plan, many of them by following Dave's baby steps to building financial wealth, and they worked the plan. That plan included living on a monthly budget, investing in mutual funds and/or real estate, and paying cash for necessities, wants, and desires. Most of them are self-described evangelical Christians who tithe like I do, giving 10 percent or more of their net worth to their churches.

Here's where it gets interesting. Eighty percent of the people who call in to the show say that after they got out of debt and started building wealth, they started increasing their giving. That's the place I look forward to getting to. Let me share my blueprint for giving and, Lord willing, people who read this and share a like vision will give me the help for the dream to come to pass: I am going to create summer camps for student athletes—camps that use the steps in this book as a curriculum. In addition to teaching young folks athletic skills, we will teach them how to identify their gift and give them the training they will need to use their gift to serve others and make a living.

Although I have a PhD and I'm a college professor, I think there's way too much emphasis on defining success as earning a college degree. I recently heard a scholar say that this emphasis on everybody needing to go to college dates to the days of the Clinton White House of the 1990s. Although it's a well-meaning public policy message, it has led to several generations of people taking on government-subsidized student loans on the Sallie Mae program and going to college. I was part of that exodus out of a small town, heading to a college town with no clue of what I was going to do for years. Here we are, almost twenty years later, and most young folks at college have no clue why they're there other than that's what we do in this country. Even the folks who decide to go into the military first often do so in hopes of taking advantage of the GI Bill, which pays for veterans' education. But again, they have no clue why they're going to college. When you ask them why, they respond that they don't know.

My plan is to create as many different ways as possible to help people identify their gifts and then, most importantly, help them figure out the best space for them to get prepared to use their gifts over the course of their lifetime. For some of you, your calling will require a degree program. But others need vocational training if they're going to serve others with their gifts and make a good income. Let me tell you something, folks: The most challenging thing that I have found since I bought my first home has been finding skilled and ethical people to do renovations and repairs. I have paid large amounts of money to plumbers, electricians, carpenters, workers, brick and stone people skilled in masonry work, tree specialists, and landscapers. I was happy to pay the good ones. But I can tell you there is a serious shortage of people who can do those jobs. My dad was one of those who came from the generation of folks who could do just about everything. Remember we used to call them Jack of all trades and master of none? You can make some great money if you have the gifts and ability to work with your hands.

What I do is not for everyone. I spend most of my time staring at a screen indoors, writing, researching, grading, sitting in meetings, and then the gravy—teaching students. For some folks, that would drive them crazy! What we would do at the camp is to identify opportunities to expose young people to different types of jobs and have experts come in and speak to them, giving the students an opportunity to ask questions. Here's a tip for you right now. One of the best ways for you to learn about a career that you may have some interest in is to do a career interview with somebody experienced in that field. You ask questions such as, "If you were starting over, what kind of training do you think is essential to do your job? What are the things that you love about your job? What are the things that you don't like?" Too often, we fantasize about what it's like to do a particular job. I always tell people that if you want to be a teacher I don't have to prepare you for the gravy, which is teaching students. I have to prepare you for grading papers, campus meetings, and committee work. That's the part of our career that my wife and I, both college professors, don't like and have to get psyched up to do.

Every job has a preseason-football-like aspect to it, even the best jobs. So, at our camp, that's what we would do—get on the lacrosse field and love playing the Creator's game. And while I'm at it, let me explain my view of athletics. Taking several pages out of Joe Ehrmann's book, *InSideOut Coaching*, I think sports are a great way for young people to have fun and develop meaningful relationships with others and for each gender to learn how to be mature adults. If done right, sports can help you learn the life lessons you'll need to get ahead in the future. So, how about ways to spend time on the field learning skills and developing healthy minds and bodies. How about places with excellent food that teach people how to eat to win. I'd call on athletes like Tom Brady, LeBron James, and Carmelo Anthony—athletes who, as veterans in their sports, have recently made some radical changes to how they eat for the purpose of prolonging their careers and giving their maximum effort.

I had the pleasure of meeting former NFL offensive lineman Jason Brown while doing a speaking event in Ohio on gardening. He is a guy who left a professional football career at his prime upon hearing God's call to return to his native state of North Carolina and start First Fruits Farm. At the time, Jason knew nothing about farming, so he had to learn as much as he could, including tapping into self-help videos on YouTube and asking a lot of questions from neighboring farmers. Like me, Jason has a dream of a farm where young athletes can come learn their skills as well as all the other skills needed to keep the farm up and running. As Jason says, being in farming has meant learning plumbing, electricity, masonry work, carpentry, and so on. In addition, when you get young folks planting and harvesting the food that they eat, it expands their palate and desire for produce. That's one of the areas in which I want to give.

How about a camp that would target low-income student athletes? It would be like a domestic version of the United Nations, with children from all over the United States. Participants would have to pay a minimum amount to attend the two-week summer camp, which would conclude with participation in a tournament in their sport. They would pay enough so that I know they have some skin in the game. I want them to invest in their future. I know several teachers and coaches with whom I've shared my vision who are ready to jump in and give their time. That's part of living and giving like no one else—the ability to drop what you're doing and give of your time.

Give of your time to Habitat for Humanity, an organization of volunteers that builds homes for people in need around the United States and the world. Give to Doctors Without Borders, which goes to areas during crisis situations, donating their medical skills to help treat people who would not normally be able to receive necessary medical care. Give time on long- or short-term missionary trips to places like Haiti and Syria. These are just a few opportunities in which you could give time and money.

I tell audiences when I give talks that you should be in the position in which you create your monthly budget and you include gifts in it. You keep, say, $600 cash, and you meet needs as God leads you to see them. For instance, set up scholarship funds for kids at community colleges to pay for their books and tuition based on a category that you decide. Professors like me have books stacked up in our offices that we no longer use. I know a private school in Sierra Leone, Africa, where I like to ship these books. What about finding a nonprofit that collects books from your community and finds places that need them around the world? Doing stuff like that makes me feel good. People say money's not everything, and I agree, but I can do a whole lot more good when I have more money than when I don't.

These are just some of the thoughts that come to mind when I think of the concept of living and giving like no one else. Aren't you tired of being normal, which, in most instances, means broke and selfish? I'm laying out a vision for you and I hope you grab it and run with it. It starts with implementing what I have shared in this book. You also might want to look at my forthcoming book, *The Super Seven: Principles for Planning Success.* I wrote the book to explain how I succeeded both on and off the field despite having a severe learning disability, and, quite frankly, being a black male in a society that doesn't hold black males in high esteem and expects the worst from us. Before getting mad at what I said, ask yourself, if you're not one, would you want to trade places with the average black male in American society?

I laid out my super seven in response to the question, do you want to succeed on purpose and make it a formula rather than an oops-look-what-happened-to-me scenario. As I like to say, success and failure are both planned events. If a student comes to me and says, "I need an A in your class so I don't fail out of school," I don't say, but I think, "You did a whole lot of activity and planning to get to this point, and it's got nothing to do with my class." In my experience, success is 80 percent perspiration and 20 percent inspiration. It's about putting in the time necessary to achieve your SMART goal.

Too many people need to go back to the beginning and start with what their gift is. What's the thing that you do better than everybody else, with less effort? If you can start with investigating that question, it will make the rest of your journey enjoyable and understandable. We have too many people who are clueless about what they should be doing, jumping from one opportunity to another based on compensation. In the process, they are making themselves and those around them miserable. My message is: Why not take the steps and the time necessary to make your vocation feel like a vacation?

# AFTERWORD

I hope you enjoyed reading this book is much as I did writing it. The process has forced me to put on paper a lot of things that I have been thinking about but have not shared with others. In many ways, this book is about stewardship. It's about being a good steward of the gifts that God has given you and it's about being a good steward of the resources you have.

This is also a book about honor. One of the themes that I share is that work—all work—is honorable. We need to move away from prioritizing college-educated work and embrace those of us with all kinds of skills, gifts, and abilities. The bottom line is that we need one another. We all bring something to the table that everyone needs.

We also need to break the stereotypes that are associated with the trades. The way it stands now, most of the trades are very gender-centered and, as a result, gifted women feel uncomfortable entering them and believe they need to act like tomboys. In addition, those in the trades don't have a pass on reading and learning about the kind of topics that those of us have access to when we get a liberal arts education. Learning how to be a good citizen is just as important as being highly skilled. Similarly, we don't get a pass on financial literacy. I think this is even more important for those in the trades because many of you are entrepreneurs. Those who are college-educated don't get a pass on understanding the basics you need for using a screwdriver, hammer, or saw. Everybody needs basic skills, and by learning them you'll save a ton of money on necessary home maintenance and repairs.

We also need to reeducate ourselves as a society so that we end not only the gender biases that exist in occupations but also the ethnic biases in which some ethnic groups feel more welcome in certain fields than others. This comes from years and years of miseducation that needs to be challenged. I am promoting some of the principles that Booker T. Washington incorporated into the curriculum of Tuskegee Institute—the ideal of a self-contained, work-study type of college education. In many ways it is what they do at Northeastern University, where students spend an entire semester in internships combined with classes. There is much to be praised in this model.

Now let me share my last observation and suggestion. I think mandatory military service will be another thing that is good for our country. There a lot of skills and self-discipline that one acquires from military service. I think it would also make us think twice before we put the most impoverished among our citizens in harm's way as enlistees in our armed forces. We could transform the armed forces into a system for instilling an understanding of one's gifts, self-discipline, and courage and for skill training for the essentials that we need as a society to continue to strive for. We need more of a hybrid educational system that embraces the best of a liberal arts education and a vocational education, and I think in many ways that's what Booker T. Washington attempted to do at Tuskegee.

The whole debate about what's more important—a liberal arts education or vocational training—I believe is moot when one considers the primacy of understanding your God-given gift, knowing that your gift is a starting place for what you can give back to society, and being well compensated in the process. We need your gift, we need your gift, we need your gift! It doesn't matter to me if you don't know what it is. It's still in you, and we need to help you get it out so you can make an important contribution to the world around you and be well compensated in the process.

Thank you for taking the time to read this book. I pray that you will share it with others.

Fred Opie
Natick, Massachusetts, 2017

# ABOUT THE AUTHOR

Fred Opie, aka Dr. Frederick Douglass Opie, is an author, college professor, podcaster, and coach. Opie has appeared on NPR, BBC Radio, the History Channel, and PBS television. He played lacrosse at Syracuse University and on a US men's national team. He has served on the Board of Directors of US Lacrosse and MetroLacrosse.

## Other Published Works

*Southern Food and Civil Rights: Feeding the Revolution* (American Palate Series)

*Zora Neale Hurston on Florida Food: Recipes, Remedies, and Simple Pleasures* (American Palate Series)

*Upsetting the Apple Cart: Black and Latino Coalitions in New York from Protest to Public Office* (Columbia History of Urban Life Series, ed. Kenneth Jackson, Columbia University Press)

*Black Labor Migration in Caribbean Guatemala, 1882-1923* (Florida Work in the Americas Series, University of Florida Press)

*Hog and Hominy: Soul Food from Africa to America* (Arts and Traditions of the Table: Perspectives on Culinary History Series, ed. Albert Sonnenfeld, Columbia University Press)

# INDEX

# NOTES

1. Joe Ehrmann, *Inside Out Coaching: How Sports Can Transform Lives* (New York: Simon & Schuster, 2011), 93.
2. Kevin Leman, *Planet Middle School: Helping Your Child through the Peer Pressure, Awkward Moments & Emotional Drama* (Grand Rapids: Revell, 2015).
3. Simon Sinek, *Start with Why: How Great Leaders Inspire Everyone to Take Action* (New York: Portfolio, 2009).
4. Bobby Orr, *Orr: My Story* (New York: G. P. Putnam's Sons, 2013).
5. Listen to Canadian national team director Dave Huntley share his story about seeing Wayne Gretzky play lacrosse before he went on to a pro career in the NHL. Huntley grew up in Canada playing hockey before gaining All-American honors as a Johns Hopkins University lacrosse player. Here's a link to the podcast on *The Fred Opie Show*: www.soundcloud.com/fredopieshow/acanadiansjourneyfromhockeytohopkinslacrosse
6. Steve Harvey, *Act Like a Success, Think Like a Success: Discovering Your Gifts and the Way to Life's Riches* (New York: Amistad, 2014), 68–73.
7. Ibid.
8. Frederick Douglass, *Narrative of the Life of Frederick Douglass, An American Slave, Written by Himself* (Chapel Hill, NC: Academic Affairs Library, University of North Carolina at Chapel Hill, 1999 [originally published 1845]), www.docsouth.unc.edu/neh/douglass/douglass.html.
9. Malcolm X, *The Autobiography of Malcolm X*, with the assistance of Alex Haley, introduced by M. S. Handler, epilogue by Alex Haley (New York: Ballantine Books, 1964).
10. Zig Ziglar, *Better Than Good: Creating a Life You Can't Wait to Live* (Nashville: Thomas Nelson, 2001), 207.

11. Harvey, *Act Like a Success*, 72.

12. Ibid., 77.

13. Martin Kessler, "'Nobody Who Looks Like You Is On TV:' The Story of A Sikh Broadcaster," *Only a Game*, NPR, April 28, 2017; NPR online blog post and podcast, April 28, 2017.

14. Mike Woicik, *Total Conditioning for Football: The Syracuse Way*, (Champaign, Illinois Human Kinetics, 1985).

15. So, what's a dissertation? I'm glad you asked: a paper project that is in the social sciences such as history, is several chapters long, and book length. It's based on one's original research, and in my case, research done in the archives in Guatemala City, Guatemala, as well as the national archives in College Park, Maryland, and various other archives around the country. It's an exercise that, after I reconsider it many years later, it introduced me to how to write a book. There are lots of people who go to graduate school, enter PhD programs, and finish all of the requirements except for writing and completing the dissertation. In graduate school, we call this being ABD—all but the dissertation. It's a status that you're excited about getting to but not one you want to stay in more than one or two years. Being ABD for more than that is like being in jail waiting to go on trial. It's not that bad, but it sure feels like it when you're in it.

16. Books I have enjoyed on the topic of mentoring and which have influenced my thoughts on the topic in this book include: Denzel Washington, *A Hand to Guide Me: Legends and Leaders Celebrate The People Who Shaped Their Lives* (Des Moines, Iowa: Meredith Books; 1st edition, 2006); Tony Dungy with Nathan Whitaker and Jim Caldwell, *The Mentor Leader: Secrets to Building People & Teams That Win Consistently* (Carol Stream, Illinois: Tyndale House Publishers Inc., 2011); Matilda Raffa Cuomo, *The Person Who Changed My Life: Prominent People Recall Their Mentors* (New York: Rodale; Revised. Edition, 2011); Dr. Henry Cloud, *The Power of the Other: The Startling Effect Other People Have on You, from the Boardroom to the Bedroom and Beyond—and What to Do about It* (New York: Harper Business, 2016).

17. Joan E. McLachlan and Patricia F. Hess, *Get an Internship and Make the Most of It: Practical Information for High School and Community College Students* (Lanham, MD: Rowman & Littlefield, 2015).

18. McLachlan and Hess, *Get an Internship*, 77–82.

19. Ibid., 74–75.

20. Rachel Bridge, *You Can Do It Too: The 20 Essential Things Every Budding Entrepreneur Should Know* (London: Kogan Page, 2010), 29.

21. Bridge, *You Can Do It Too*, 30–31.

22. Dawn M. Baskerville, "Get a Mentor: The Right Ways to Choose and Schmooze a Savvy Career Adviser," *Black Enterprise* (May 1994), 44.

23. Dave Ramsey, "The Billionaire and the Money Mentor," www.daveramsey.com/blog/the-billionaire-and-the-money-mentor.

24. By the way, while writing this book, I came across some great books on the topic of the teenage brain and frontal cortex that I would highly recommend you check out: Dr. Jeramy Clark and Jerusha Clark, *Your Teenager Is Not Crazy: Understanding Your Teen's Brain Can Make You a Better Parent* (Ada, Michigan: Baker Books, 2016); Eric Jensen and Carole Snider, *Turnaround Tools for the Teenage Brain: Helping Underperforming Students Become Lifelong Learners* (New York: Jossey-Bass, 2013); Frances E. Jensen and Amy Ellis Nutt, *The Teenage Brain: A Neuroscientist's Survival Guide to Raising Adolescents and Young Adults* (New York: Harper Paperbacks, 2016).

25. Jensen and Snider, *Turnaround Tools for the Teenage Brain*, 21–22; Jensen and Ellis Nutt, *The Teenage Brain*, 13, 35–36.

26. Harry J. Holzer, "Better Skills for Better Jobs," *Issues in Science and Technology* 28, no. 2 (2012), 32–35; Philip Oreopoulos and Uros Petronijevic, "Making College Worth It: A Review of the Returns to Higher Education," *The Future of Children* 23, no. 1 (2013), 58.

27. Megan M. Holland and Stefanie DeLuca, "'Why Wait Years to Become Something?' Low-Income African American Youth and the Costly Career Search in For-Profit Trade Schools," *Sociology of Education* 89, no. 4 (2016), 262, 273.

28. Oreopoulos and Petronijevic, "Making College Worth It," 45.

29. Ibid., 53–55.

30. Oreopoulos and Petronijevic, "Making College Worth It," 58–59, 61.

31. Manuel S. González Canché, "Is the Community College a Less Expensive Path toward a Bachelor's Degree?: Public 2- and 4-Year Colleges' Impact on Loan Debt," *The Journal of Higher Education* 85, no. 5 (2014), 752.

32. Thomas Snyder, *The Community College Career Track: How to Achieve the American Dream without a Mountain of Debt* (Somerset, NJ: John Wiley & Sons, 2012), 14, 32.

33. Ibid.

34. Sarah A. Beamer, "Private vs. Public Higher Education Budgeting," *Planning for Higher Education* 40, no. 1 (2011), 9.

35. Ibid.
36. Kim Clark, "Three Ways to Help Your Clients Make Smart College Choices," *The Journal of Financial Planning* (April 2016), 29–30.
37. Dave Ramsey, *The Total Money Makeover: Classic Edition: A Proven Plan for Financial Fitness* (Nashville: Thomas Nelson, 2013), 157–160.
38. Malcolm Gladwell, *Outliers: The Story of Success* (New York: Little Brown, 2008), Chapter 2.
39. McLachlan and Hess, *Get an Internship*, viii.
40. McLachlan and Hess, *Get an Internship*, 84.
41. McLachlan and Hess, *Get an Internship*, 86.
42. Ibid., 87.
43. Stephen King, *On Writing: 10th Anniversary Edition: A Memoir of the Craft* (New York: Scribner, 10th Anniversary Edition, 2010).
44. McLachlan and Hess, *Get an Internship*, 87.
45. Jim Dent, *The Junction Boys: How Ten Days in Hell with Bear Bryant Forged a Championship Team* (New York: St. Martin's Griffin, 2000).
46. Beverly Bachel, "Best Internship Ever! Here's How to Get the Most Out of Your On-the-Job Experience," *Career World (Weekly Reader)* 36, no. 5 (2008).
47. Beverly Bachel, "Best Internship Ever!"
48. Martin Kessler, "'Nobody Who Looks Like You Is On TV:' The Story of A Sikh Broadcaster," *Only a Game*, NPR, April 28, 2017; NPR online blog post and podcast, April 28, 2017.
49. Originally aired April 29, 2016 on NPR's *Morning Edition*.
50. Originally aired March 31, 2017 on NPR's *Morning Edition*.
51. Bill Hybels, *Simplify: 10 Practices to Unclutter Your Soul* (Carol Stream, Illinois: Tyndale House Publishers, 2014), 84–86.
52. Ibid., 107–108.

Made in the USA
Middletown, DE
27 June 2021

42980421R00066